An Introduction to Deep Reinforcement Learning

The current era of artificial intelligence and machine learning (AIML) tools has transformed the workings of vast swaths of our private, working, and social lives beyond recognition. It has been found that these tools can solve many problems in better and faster ways compared to humans. AIML tools allow machines and related systems to reason and infer almost like humans, and this has deep intellectual and philosophical ramifications as well. The areas of machine learning are broadly classified into supervised, unsupervised, and deep reinforcement learning (DRL). The last one comes closest to how humans reason, and various innovations in this area have many useful applications.

This book covers most of the areas of DRL, with a special focus on its mathematical and algorithmic foundations. Undergraduate and early graduate students should find it to be a good guide to the fast-developing areas of DRL and its myriad applications in both technical and social contexts.

Vinod K. Mishra received his PhD in Theoretical Physics from the State University of New York (SUNY) at Stony Brook. After gaining some academic teaching and research experience, he joined Lucent Technology Bell Labs and later became a research scientist at US Army Research Laboratory. His areas of primary interest are quantum information science, artificial intelligence, and machine learning. He is the author of *An Introduction to Quantum Communication* and *Software Defined Networks*.

An Introduction to Deep Reinforcement Learning

Vinod K. Mishra

CRC Press
Taylor & Francis Group
Boca Raton London New York

CRC Press is an imprint of the
Taylor & Francis Group, an **informa** business
A CHAPMAN & HALL BOOK

Designed cover image: Shutterstock

ATLAB® and Simulink® are trademarks of The MathWorks, Inc. and are used with permission. The MathWorks does not warrant the accuracy of the text or exercises in this book. This book's use or discussion of MATLAB® or Simulink® software or related products does not constitute endorsement or sponsorship by The MathWorks of a particular pedagogical approach or particular use of the MATLAB® and Simulink® software.

First edition published 2026
by CRC Press
2385 NW Executive Center Drive, Suite 320, Boca Raton FL 33431

and by CRC Press
4 Park Square, Milton Park, Abingdon, Oxon, OX14 4RN

CRC Press is an imprint of Taylor & Francis Group, LLC

© 2026 Vinod K. Mishra

ISBN: 978-1-032-65979-4 (hbk)
ISBN: 978-1-032-65143-9 (pbk)
ISBN: 978-1-032-65980-0 (ebk)

DOI: 10.1201/9781032659800

Typeset in Minion
by Newgen Publishing UK

Contents

Prologue

THE IDEA OF PUTTING INFORMATION IN A DIGITAL FORM is quite simple and seems an ordinary technical advance in hindsight. Over a period, many scientists and engineers nurtured it at a steady pace, and finally made it possible for the society to usher in the age of digital revolution. In a relatively very short time by historical standards, it has transformed the modern civilization and changed the workings of vast swaths of our private, working, and social lives beyond recognition. The idea of machine learning has been one of the key innovations in this regard.

Machines, specifically those which can think and act like humans, have been the stuff of science fiction for a long time. At some deeper level, this concept also connects to our quest for understanding the essence of human intelligence and consciousness. We are still very far from solving that puzzle, but the impulse has resulted in very rapid advances in the fields of machine learning. We have also found that these thinking machines can solve many problems in better and faster ways compared to humans.

This book presents a high-level view of the fast developing discipline of the Reinforcement Learning in its basic and more sophisticated aspects. Hopefully, it will inspire the reader to take a deeper dive into this subject as well as help understand the coming revolution in every aspect of society based on these ideas.

CHAPTER 1

Introduction

IN THIS CHAPTER, SOME basic concepts behind machine learning (ML) and their history have been presented.

1.1 ARTIFICIAL INTELLIGENCE (AI)

AI uses data input, computing hardware, and appropriate software to model the underlying neural circuits mimicking human learning and problem-solving behavior. It has excelled at some of the learning and reasoning tasks and surpassed human capabilities.

A general AI system contains two basic layers.

  i. Infrastructure layer:

    • Central processing unit (CPU) for serially executed tasks,

- Graphics processing unit (GPU) for graphics and image calculations),
- Dedicated AI chips like Google's tensor processing unit (TPU) chips, and
- High-speed networks behind frameworks like Tensorflow, Caffe, Mxnet, Torch, Keras, PyTorch, Theano, etc.

ii. Algorithm layer: It contains various types of ML algorithms which will be elaborated in coming chapters.

1.2 MACHINE LEARNING

In recent times the field of ML has developed very fast and has branched into many subfields. The following are the most recognized ML methods.

- *Supervised Learning:* Labeled data is given as input for learning.
- *Unsupervised Learning:* Unlabeled data is given as input for learning. The combination of unsupervised and supervised learning is called *semi-supervised learning* in which both labeled and unlabeled data are given as input.
- *Reinforcement Learning (RL):* Learning is based on intelligent agents taking actions to maximize the cumulative reward from environments.

Neural networks (NNs) model neurons as electronic circuits and use them as their basic building blocks. They perform *deep learning* (DL) when the number of NN layers is increased. Further classification is determined by these basic methods:

i. *Back Propagation NN (BPNN)*
   The NN circuit signals are used to update earlier layer, a key discovery behind the NN revolution.

ii. *Convolutional NN (CNN)*

It uses the mathematical operation of convolution (an integral or sum expressing the amount of overlap of one function with shifted another function) instead of matrix multiplication in at least one of its layers, and

iii. *Recurrent NN (RNN)*

The connections between nodes form a directed graph along a temporal sequence.

The following are some of the important, but nonexhaustive NN types based on the above paradigms:

i. *Feedforward Neural Networks (FFNN):* They are the most basic type of NN consisting of an input layer, one or more hidden layers, and an output layer, with the data flowing sequentially through them from the input to the output layer. They are widely used for image and speech recognition, natural language processing, and predictive modeling. In an FFNN, each neuron in the hidden layer(s) applies an activation function to a weighted sum of the inputs and passes the output to the next layer. Their weights and biases get adjusted during the training to minimize the errors between the predicted and the actual output.

ii. *Perceptron:* It is a single-layer NN that takes a set of inputs, processes them, and produces an output. They apply weights to the input data and then pass the sum through an activation function to produce an output. The activation function is typically a threshold function that outputs a 1 or 0 depending on whether the sum is above or below a certain threshold. They are used for image recognition, signal processing, and control systems and are somewhat limited in their applications as they can only solve linearly separable problems in which the data can be separated into two categories using a straight line.

iii. *Multilayer Perceptron (MLP):* It is a type of FFNN commonly used for classification tasks. The input layer receives the raw data. Each following MLP layer consists of many perceptrons, and the output of one MLP layer feeds into the next layer as input. The hidden layers in between transform the input into a form that is suitable for the output layer, which produces the final prediction. MLPs have been applied to image recognition, speech recognition, time series analysis, and natural language processing.

iv. *Recurrent Neural Networks (RNN):* They process sequential input data, such as text and speech The input data is processed through a series of recurrent neurons, which take the current input and the output from the previous time step as input, thus allowing the network to maintain a memory of previous inputs and context. The weights and biases of the neurons are adjusted during training to minimize the error between the predicted output and the actual output – a process called back propagation. RNNs are commonly used for language translation, text generation, speech recognition, and time series prediction.

v. *Long Short-Term Memory (LSTM):* It is a type of RNN for handling long-term dependencies and contains memory cells, input gates, output gates, and forget gates.

The information flows through the memory cells over time. The input and forget gates determine which information should be stored in the memory cells and which information should be removed. The output gate then determines which information should be passed on to the next layer. Thus, LSTM remembers important information over long periods of time and selectively forgets irrelevant information. They have solved problems with long-term dependencies effectively in natural language processing, speech recognition, handwriting recognition, and other applications where long-term memory is important.

vi. *Radial Basis Function (RBF) Neural Network:* It is an FFNN that uses a set of RBFs to transform its inputs into outputs. It is composed of an input layer, a hidden layer, and an output layer. It uses a set of RBFs to transform the input data by calculating the distance between the input and a set of predefined centers in the hidden layer. The hidden layer outputs are then combined linearly to produce the final output. The weights of the connections between the hidden and the output layer are trained using a supervised learning algorithm, such as backpropagation. RBF networks are often used for problems with large datasets as they learn to generalize well and provide good predictions. They are used for time-series analysis and prediction, financial forecasting, pattern recognition, classification, and control tasks.

vii. *Convolutional Neural Networks (CNN):* These are made up of convolutional, pooling, and fully connected layers. The input data is processed through many convolutional layers, which apply filters to the input and extract features. Their output then passes through pooling layers, which down-sample the data to reduce its dimension. Finally, the output goes through fully connected layers for the final classification or prediction. The CNNs are commonly used for image and video recognition tasks, such as object detection, facial recognition, and self-driving cars.

viii. *Autoencoder:* This NN uses unsupervised learning which does not require labeled data to make predictions. It first compresses the input data into a lower-dimensional representation and then reconstructs it back into the original format, thus identifying the most important features of the input data. They are commonly used in applications such as data compression, feature extraction, image denoising, and anomaly detection. For example, NASA uses them to detect anomalies in spacecraft sensor data.

ix. *Sequence to Sequence Models (Seq2Seq):* They use an encoder and a decoder to convert one sequence of data into another by first encoding the input sequence into a fixed-length vector. Then the decoder uses this vector to generate the output sequence one element at a time, predicting the next element based on the previous one and the context vector. These models have been used in natural language processing, machine translation, conversational agents, and language translations.

x. *Modular Neural Network (MNN):* In MNN, each module is a separate network for solving a specific subproblem, and all module outputs are then combined to provide a final output. This approach makes it easier to build complex systems by combining simpler modules. They can be more robust than traditional NNs, as each module can handle a specific type of input or noise, so that even if one module fails, the overall system can still function, as other modules can take over. MNNs have been used in computer vision, speech recognition, and robotics.

1.3 APPLICATIONS OF AI

Attempts to understand the nature of intelligence started a long time ago and various ancient cultures – e.g. Greek, Indian, Chinese, and others – produced many philosophical ideas about it. Later tools of mathematics, logic, and engineering ushered us in the current era of new understanding and applications.

The field of AI is very broad, with a nonexhaustive list of subfields given below.

i. *Neural Networks:* Study the promise and limitations of computational networking based on neuron models, e.g., brain modeling, time series prediction, classification, etc.

ii. *Evolutionary Computation:* Study and development of computer programs correcting and improving themselves automatically without human intervention during execution, e.g., genetic programming, etc.

iii. *Vision:* Developing machines to understand and interpret the visual input, e.g., object recognition, image understanding, etc.

iv. *Robotics*: Building machines capable of autonomous movement, e.g., intelligent control, autonomous exploration, etc.

v. *Expert Systems*: Software embodying the facts and rules of a particular area of knowledge, e.g., decision support systems, teaching systems, etc.

vi. *Speech Processing*: Development of systems able to understand naturally spoken languages, e.g., speech recognition and processing.

vii. *Natural Language Processing:* Extraction of meaning and structure of the written or printed natural languages, e.g., machine translation.

viii. *Planning:* Using current data to enumerate steps to achieve a well-defined goal, e.g., scheduling, etc.

ix. *Machine Learning:* Study and development of machines and algorithms capable of learning, e.g., decision trees, etc.

The new areas for using neural networks are always opening.

1.4 HISTORICAL DEVELOPMENT

A short history based on the milestones follows based on Royal Society (UK) Report [1].

i. *18th Century:*

- Development of statistical methods which accelerated the pace of scientific research in general.
- *Bayes' Theorem (1763):* Usually we have some prior knowledge of the conditions leading to an event. This theorem relates them.

$$P(A|B) = \frac{P(B|A)P(A)}{P(B)} \quad (1.1)$$

Here $P(A)$ and $P(B)$ are the probabilities of the occurrence of events A and B independently. $P(A|B)$ and $P(B|A)$ are conditional probabilities of occurrence of event A or B given that B or A is true. This simple relation has played an outsized role in the development of AI/ML.

ii. *1950s:*

- *Turing Test (1950):* Alan Turing presented the criteria by which machines can be considered intelligent if its responses to questions could convince a person that it is human.
- Checker playing machine (1952): Arthur Samuel created a machine able to learn to pay checkers using expert rules and playing against itself.
- Dartmouth workshop (1956): This was a get-together of the AI/ML's early pioneers. John McCarthy came up with the term 'Artificial Intelligence.'

- The Perceptron (1957): Frank Rosenblatt invented the first 'neural network' using a potentiometer and an electric motor. It could take an input (like a pixel) and create an output (like a label).

iii. *1960s and 1970s:* not much, AI winter

iv. *1980s:*

- 'Parallel Distributed Processing' in two volumes (1986): advocated the use of NN models for ML

v. *1990s:*

- Backgammon playing neural network algorithm (1992): Gerald Tesauro created a backgammon playing program based on NN, which could match the best human players.
- Deep Blue beats world chess champion (1997): It could process 200 million moves per second before selecting the best one.

vi. *2010s:*

- IBM's Watson beats Jeopardy champion (2011):
- ImageNet (2012): A paper by Alex Krizhevsky, Ilya Sutskever, and Geoffrey Hinton presented a model that dramatically reduced the error rate in image recognition systems.
- AlphaGo beats Go champion (2016): Program created by Google's DeepMind team won four out of five games against Chinese master of Go game.
- Libratus beats poker champion (2017): Program created by Carnegie Mellon University beat top poker player, and this success was repeated by University of Alberta's program Deepstack.
- Transformer architecture: The Google researchers published a paper 'Attention is all you need' (2017)

starting a new and powerful approach to large language models (LLMs).

- Development of foundational LLM models (2018) trained on vast amounts of unlabeled data started.

vii. *2020s:*

- GPT-3 was released by OpenAI (2020).
- GPT-4 was released by Microsoft (2023). It is a milestone toward achieving a 'General AI' system.

1.5 SOME GENERAL REMARKS

The new technologies have always created great hopes and fears in society and AI/ML is not an exception. In addition, it has raised some philosophical questions about the essence of human uniqueness. We discuss some of them without giving definite answers.

The human brain consists of about 86 billion neurons and 100 trillion synapses which often fire asynchronously in parallel. Furthermore, it runs on less than 20 watts of power, making it one of its kind in the natural world. On the other hand, the number of neurons in an artificial neural network (ANN) is somewhere between 100 and 1,000. It has been found that increasing their numbers does not necessarily improve the network performance. Also in ANN, only the neighboring layers are connected which, in most cases, are activated sequentially, and it usually consumes about 200 watts and also produces heat.

All of this points to the fact that a huge improvement in the architecture and algorithms of ANN is needed before they can be comparable to the brain. Still the progress has been remarkable so far and is accelerating fast.

Our intelligence has many components and a few of them like recognizing outside objects and events and their understanding are one of them. This involves comparing new information against the older stored ones. The AI through neural networks also works like that. The NN is trained on known cases and that training is used for recognizing or classifying the new data. This aspect of human intelligence has been well captured by the machines and they can be said to have even surpassed us. This has been demonstrated by machines beating humans, for example, in games of chess and Go. It seems that machines will surpass humans in all such situations sooner or later where this paradigm is applicable.

Robotics combined with AI is another area where machines will outperform humans. This is just the extension of the situations in which traditional machines like cars, planes, and other similar inventions extend human capabilities. The working of AI/ML algorithms in real time becomes visible through machine movements and that is something new. This has generated in general public's mind more fear and curiosity than anything else.

The ANN may also give new insights to better understand the brain by studying how it generates its outputs and changes in response to new input. That may well provide useful insights into their working of human and other biological brains. So, while ANNs are far from being able to replicate the brain functions in totality, they can still help us solve complex problems such as optimizing logistics for transportation networks and processing raw photos and videos in medical imaging, robotics, or facial recognition.

It is still not clear how moral and ethical concerns can be encoded in the AI/ML algorithms right from the beginning.

CHAPTER 2

Survey of ML

AFTER THE ADVENT OF the machine learning (ML) paradigm, many different approaches to ML were quickly
discovered. They are often characterized as being with or
without deep learning (DL), a very important part of AI/ML.

DL provides a method for approximating arbitrary functions
in high-dimensional feature space (corresponding to large
number of independent features) using NN. It uses input data
as examples and learns the data's structure and functional
relationships among its features using various algorithms based
on the statistical methods such as linear regression, decision
trees (DT), random forests (RF), support vector machines
(SVMs), artificial neural networks (ANNs), boosting, etc. An
input layer followed by analysis and an output layer is sometimes called 'shallow learning.'

 DOI: 10.1201/9781032659800-2

In contrast, 'deep learning' has one or more hidden layers between input and output layers. At each layer (except input layer), the following action steps take place:

- At the current layer, the weighted sum of units from the previous layer is computed.
- A nonlinear transformation or an activation function (e.g., logistic function, hyperbolic tangent, rectified linear unit (ReLU), etc.) is applied to the sum.
- This sum and weights on the inter-layer links become the input to the next layer.

This way, the computations flow forward from input layer to the output layer. For backpropagation, at output layer and each hidden layer, one computes the error derivatives backward, and backpropagates gradients toward the input layer. The weights are then updated to optimize some chosen loss function.

This basic approach is used in many ways to accomplish various ML tasks. Some of these approaches are the focus of this chapter.

2.1 LEARNING FROM PROBLEMS

One way of learning starts from a problem and learns the methods, techniques, and steps for solving it from known methods of solution. Here we provide a nonexhaustive list of the main varieties of this approach (Table 2.1).

2.1.1 Supervised (or Discriminative) Learning

In this approach, labeled historical or experimental data is used as input for learning. Labels are tagged by experts and contain descriptive features (attributes taking either numerical or binary values) and target features (desired information). The learning is also called 'classification' for discrete and 'regression' for continuous labels. The ML techniques are used to learn

TABLE 2.1 Varieties of Machine Learning: Learning from Problems

Supervised (or Discriminative) Learning	**(A representative list)**
	- Multi-layer perceptron (MLP):
	  i. Feed-forward MLP (FF-MLP)
	  ii. Back-propagation MLP (BP-MLP)
	- Convolutional NN (CNN)
	- Recurrent NN (RNN):
	  i. Long short-term memory (LSTM)
	  ii. Bidirectional LSTM (Bi-LSTM)
	  iii. Gated Recurrent Unit (GRU)

Semi-supervised Learning	Applicable when data labels are missing or incomplete

Unsupervised (or Generative) Learning	**(A representative list)**
	- Generative adversarial network (GAN)
	- Restricted Boltzmann machine (RBM)
	- Radial basis function network (RBFN)
	- Self-organizing map (SOM)
	- Auto-encoder (AE):
	  i. Sparse AE (SAE)
	  ii. Denoising AE (DAE)
	  iii. Contractive AE (CAE)
	  iv. Variational AE (VAE)
	- Deep belief network (DBN)

Self-supervised Learning	Intermediate between unsupervised and supervised learning

Hybrid Learning	- Integrate more than one of either variety (generative or discriminative)
	  i. CNN+LSTM,
	  ii. AE+GAN, etc.
	- Generative stack followed by discriminative stack.
	  i. DBN+MLP,
	  ii. GAN+CNN,
	  iii. AE+CNN, etc.
	- Integrate either variety with non-deep learning classifier.
	  i. AE+SVM,
	  ii. CNN+SVM, etc.

Deep Transfer Learning **Multi-instance Learning**	

their functional relationship and this step usually takes much time and expense. Then, the trained learning system is used to assign the new incoming data to appropriate target classes.

Some well-known but not exhaustive supervised learning algorithms are given below.

2.1.1.1 Multilayer Perceptron (MLP)

A feedforward MLP is a simpler version of artificial neural network. It is a next-level progression of single-layer perceptrons, which can distinguish only linearly separable data.

An MLP consists of at least three layers of fully connected neurons and maps a set of input values to output values. It uses a nonlinear activation function (usually a Heaviside step function) at each individual layer which can be combined to express any mathematical function in principle. It can distinguish data that is linearly nonseparable. Backpropagation algorithm is used to train them and that requires the use of continuous activation functions, e.g., sigmoid or ReLU. The MLP components and their roles are as follows:

- **Input layer:** It has neurons for receiving the initial input data and each of them represents a feature or dimension of the input data. The dimensionality of the input data determines the number of neurons.

- **Hidden layer:** These are the layers between the input and output layers in which each neuron receives inputs from all other neurons in the previous layer (either the input or another hidden layer). Then the output is passed to the next layer. The number of hidden layers and the number of neurons in each of them are called hyperparameters. They are determined during the model design phase.

- **Output layer:** Neurons at this layer produce the final output of the network, and their number depends on the nature of the task. For example: (i) in binary classification, there may be either one or two neurons depending on the activation function for representing the probability of belonging to one class, (ii) in multi-class classification tasks one may require many more neurons.

- **Weights:** Neurons in adjacent layers are fully connected to each other. Each such connection has an associated weight learned during the training process determining the strength of the connection.

- **Bias neurons:** In addition to the input and hidden neurons, each layer (except the input layer) usually also has a bias neuron, giving a constant input to the next layer neurons. Bias neurons have their own weights associated with each connection, which is learned during training. They effectively shift the activation function of the neurons in the subsequent layer to learn an offset or bias in the decision boundary. By adjusting the bias neuron weights, the MLP learns to control the threshold for activation to better fit the training data.

  Note: In general machine learning, bias has another meaning, as it refers to the error introduced by approximating a real-world problem with a simplified model, thus measuring how well the model can capture the underlying patterns in the data. A high bias indicates that the model is too simplistic and may underfit the data, while a low bias suggests that the model is capturing the underlying patterns well.

- **Activation function:** Each hidden layer and the output layer neuron apply an activation function (e.g., sigmoid, tanh, ReLU, softmax, etc.) to its weighted sum of inputs. These functions introduce nonlinearity into the network, allowing it to learn complex patterns in the data.

- **Training:** MLPs are trained using the backpropagation algorithm, which computes gradients of a loss function with respect to the model's parameters. The parameters are updated iteratively to minimize the loss.

2.1.1.2 Convolutional NN (CNN)

A CNN is a feedforward deep neural network (FF-DNN), having layers with specific functions for processing data with multiple arrays, e.g., color image, language, audio spectrogram, and video. The inspiration behind CNN is the organization of neurons in our visual cortex. After the input layer, the CNN layers have the following other layers:

- *Convolutional layer*: This includes one or more layers that perform convolutions or dot product of the convolution kernel (usually Frobenius inner product with ReLU as activation function) with the layer's input matrix. This kernel slides along the input matrix and generates a feature map contributing to the input of the next layer.

- *Pooling layer:* It combines the outputs of neuron clusters at one layer into a single neuron in the next layer, thereby reducing the dimensions of data. There are two types of pooling: *max pooling* and *average pooling.* The former uses the maximum value of each local cluster of neurons in the feature map and the latter takes the average value.

- *Fully connected layers*: These layers connect every neuron in one layer to every neuron in another layer as in MLP.

2.1.1.3 Recurrent NN (RNN)

RNN uses output of the previous step as the input to the current step. In this manner, its output depends on the prior elements within the sequence. This is done with the help of hidden units which store the history of past elements using multilayer NN in which all layers have same weights. RNNs cannot store information for long time and have issues of vanishing gradients. Some of its variations are given below.

- **Long Short-Term Memory (LSTM)**

  LSTM networks (Hochreiter and Schmidhuber, 1997) and gated recurrent unit (GRU) (Chung et al., 2014) were proposed to address the vanishing gradient issue. They use gating mechanisms to manipulate information through recurrent cells. Gradient backpropagation or its variants can be used for training all deep NN. An LSTM memory cell with long period data storage capability has three gates: (i) 'Forget,' which decides which previous data will be kept or discarded; (ii) 'Input,' which controls which data enters; and (iii) 'Output,' which controls the output.

- **Bidirectional LSTM (Bi-LSTM)**

  They have two hidden layers running in opposite directions and are trained to predict negative and positive directions at the same time. It is widely used for natural language processing.

- **Gated Recurrent Unit**

  In contrast to LSTM, it has only two gates: 'Reset' and 'Update.' It does not discard information from earlier data sequence.

2.1.2 Semisupervised Learning

Semisupervised learning falls in between supervised and unsupervised learning. Many times, the desired data comes without labels or misses some of them. Sometimes, a small amount of labeled data with large number of unlabeled ones is available. Acquisition of labeled data is usually very expensive but whatever one has gives more accurate understanding of the underlying relationships. The algorithm is trained on both labeled and unlabeled data. This learning method better mimics the way humans learn.

The algorithms are a complicated mix of both supervised and unsupervised learning, e.g., generative models, low-density separation, Laplacian regularization, etc. The goal is to learn a function that can accurately predict the output variables based on the input variables, like supervised learning. Semisupervised learning builds a model with available labeled data for training and treats the rest of the unlabeled ones as test data. Some assumptions are also made implicitly by the algorithm:

- **Continuity:** The points closer to each other are more likely to have the same output label.
- **Cluster:** The data can be divided into discrete clusters and points in the same cluster are more likely to share an output label.
- **Manifold:** The data dimension is lower than that of the input space, thus allowing the use of distances and densities defined on the manifold.

2.1.3 Unsupervised (or Generative) Learning

In this approach, unlabeled data is used as input for learning, and algorithms are used to learn the patterns present in the data. These patterns capture the inherent probability densities through neural networks and statistical methods. The network mimics the given data using a learning rule and then uses the error for correcting its weights and biases. Unsupervised learning is used for tasks such as clustering, dimensionality reduction, and anomaly detection.

The sequence of actions are as follows:

- The algorithms search for frequent if-then associations to discover correlations and co-occurrences within data.
- The model learns useful data structure properties.
- Strong rules within a dataset are identified.

Some of the well-known learning rules are:

- *Hopfield learning*: A single self-connected layer mimicking the magnetic domains in iron is used. This learning layer can also be used as a content addressable memory.
- *Boltzmann machine learning*: There are two layers (hidden vs. visible) with symmetric two-way weights. Boltzmann's thermodynamics probability rule at the microscopic level is used to get at the macroscopic energies.
- *Restricted Boltzmann machine* (RBM) *learning*: This is the regular Boltzmann machine but with a restriction that lateral connections within a layer are prohibited. This makes further analysis easier.
- *Stacked RBM*: In this approach many RBMs encode hidden features hierarchically. After training a single RBM, another one is added and they are trained together again. This can go on as needed.
- *Helmholtz method*: In the stacked RBM, the bidirectional symmetric connections, separate one-way connections are used to form a loop. It does both generation and discrimination.

2.1.3.1 Generative Adversarial Network (GAN)

A GAN (Ian Goodfellow) is a type of neural network architecture for generative modeling to create new plausible samples on demand. It involves automatically discovering and learning regularities or patterns in input data so that the model may be used to generate or output new examples from the original dataset. GANs are composed of two neural networks:

- Generator G: it creates new data having properties like the original data
- Discriminator D: it predicts the likelihood of a subsequent sample being drawn from actual data rather than data provided by G.

Both *G* and *D* are trained to compete. While *G* tries to fool and confuse *D* by creating more realistic data, *D* tries to distinguish the genuine data from the fake data generated by *G*.

GAN networks are more used for unsupervised learning but have been also found useful for semisupervised, transfer, and reinforcement learning tasks. Inverse models, such as bidirectional GAN, can also learn a mapping from data to the latent space. GAN networks have been used in the areas of healthcare, image analysis, data augmentation, video generation, voice generation, pandemics, traffic control, cybersecurity, and many more.

2.1.3.2 Restricted Boltzmann Machine (RBM)

The full Boltzmann machines can learn a probability distribution from inputs. Each one of their nodes are connected to every other node. RBM is their subset which has a limit on the number of connections between the visible and hidden layers. They are more efficient for the gradient-based contrastive divergence algorithm. They can recognize patterns in data automatically to develop probabilistic models using either supervised or unsupervised learning. They have been used for dimensionality reduction, classification, regression, collaborative filtering, feature learning, topic modeling, etc.

2.1.3.3 Radial Basis Function Network (RBFN)

It is an ANN that uses radial basis functions as activation functions so that its output depends on their linear combination and neuron parameters. RBFNs are used for function approximation, time series prediction, classification, etc.

2.1.3.4 Self-Organizing Map (SOM)

SOM or Kohonen's map for unsupervised learning was introduced by Teuvo Kohonen in the 1980s. It does not use backpropagation for learning but learns by adjusting neuron weights. It reduces the dimension of data by creating a spatially organized representation.

SOMs have two layers: one for input and the other for output or the feature map. There are no activation functions as weights are passed to the output layer as they are. The dimensions of input data and of the neuron weight vector are the same. Weights are updated using the processes of competition, cooperation, and adaptation.

2.1.3.5 Autoencoder (AE)

An AE uses neural networks to learn representations for especially high-dimensional data. It has three parts:

- Encoder compresses the input.
- Code is also generated by encoder.
- Decoder uses the code to reconstruct the input.

The AEs are used for many deep learning tasks, e.g., dimensionality reduction, feature extraction, efficient coding, generative modeling, denoising, anomaly or outlier detection, etc. A single-layered AE with a linear activation function AE is like principal component analysis (PCA). AEs have many variants which are given below.

- **Sparse AE (SAE)**

  An SAE has a sparsity penalty on the coding layer. It may have more hidden units than inputs, but only a small number of them are active at the same time, thus resulting in a sparse model. They respond to the unique statistical features of the constrained training data.

- **Denoising AE (DAE)**

  This variant of AE receives a corrupted data point as input. It is trained to output the original undistorted input by minimizing the average reconstruction error over the input, thus 'denoising' it. It also alters the reconstruction criterion to make it harder to learn the identity function. DAE is very useful for automatic preprocessing of an image to boost its recognition accuracy.

- **Contractive AE (CAE)**

  CAE makes the autoencoder robust against small changes in the training dataset by including a 'regularizer' in its objective function. DAEs and CAEs make reconstruction and representation robust, respectively.

- **Variational AE (VAE)**

  A VAE is an ANN using probabilistic generative approach and was introduced by Kingma and Welling (2022). Assuming an underlying probability distribution for the source data, it tries to discover the distribution's parameters. It is very effective for generative coders for mapping the input onto a latent vector with the parameters of a probability distribution, e.g., the mean and variance of a Gaussian distribution. Initially designed for unsupervised learning, VAE has been extended to semisupervised and supervised learning.

The main components of a VAE are two NNs.

- The 'encoder,' as the first NN, maps the input data to a low-dimensional latent space of parameters of a variational distribution. It is thus able to produce many different samples coming from the same distribution.
- The second 'decoder' NN goes in the opposite direction to map the latent space to the input data space, e.g., to the means of the variational distribution. Both networks are trained together using reparameterization. Sometimes a third NN is used to map to the variance which can be optimized with gradient descent.

The model is optimized by calculating 'the reconstruction error' and 'Kullback–Leibler divergence,' which are both derived from the free energy expression of the distribution.

2.1.3.6 Deep Belief Network (DBN)

The DBN is composed of many stacked individual unsupervised networks such as AE and RBM connected sequentially. These are layers of hidden units, with connections between the layers but not between units within each layer.

Initially DBN is trained with unlabeled data and later is finetuned with labeled ones. It is good at capturing the hierarchical nature of the input and its deep patterns due to its abilities for strong feature extraction and classification. In the unsupervised learning phase, DBN learns to reconstruct its input probabilistically so that layers could act as feature detectors. Later, DBN can be further trained with supervision for the purpose of classification.

In DBN, each sub-network's hidden layer serves as the visible layer for the next. As there are connections between, but not within, layers, it leads to a fast, layer-by-layer unsupervised training.

The application of DBN in electroencephalography and drug discovery has been particularly successful.

2.1.4 Self-Supervised Learning (SSL)

SSL is a particular variation of the unsupervised learning approach. It can be also thought of as an intermediate between the supervised and unsupervised learning.

SSL learns from vast amounts of unlabeled data, so it avoids the cost of labeling and curating it. In contrast to task-specific supervised learning methods, SSL learns generic representations useful across many tasks. SSL-based models learn representations that are more robust to adversarial examples, label corruption, and input perturbations, and are fairer compared to their supervised counterparts.

There have been many recent noteworthy areas of SSL's applications.

- In natural language processing, it has led to advances from automated machine translation to large language models trained on web-scale corpus of unlabeled text. A common SSL objective is to mask a word in the text and predict the surrounding words. Finding this context allows the model to capture relationships among words in the text without the need for any labels. The same SSL model representations can be used across a range of downstream tasks such as translating text across languages, summarizing, or even generating text, etc.
- In computer vision, SSL pushed new bounds on data size with models such as SEER trained on 1 billion images. Such models have also matched or in some cases surpassed models trained on labeled data on benchmarks like ImageNet. It has also been successfully applied to video, audio, and time series by defining a pre-text task based on unlabeled inputs to produce descriptive and intelligible representations. SSL can also find two views of the same image formed by adding color or cropping, to be mapped to similar representations.

In SSL, the task is solved in two steps:

i. First the artificial neural network (ANN) is initialized with pseudo-labeled data.
ii. Using the weights and biases found in first step, the actual task is solved with either supervised or unsupervised learning.

2.1.5 Hybrid Learning

In general, we have two kinds of deep learning models:

- *Generative*: This can learn from both labeled and unlabeled data.

- *Discriminative*: This cannot learn from unlabeled data but can outperform generative on labeled data.

Hybrid networks combine the two in various ways to get the best possible results for tasks at hand.

- Approach 1: Integrate more than one of either variety, e.g., CNN+LSTM, AE+GAN, etc.

- Approach 2: Stack generative followed by discriminative, e.g., DBN+MLP, GAN+CNN, AE+CNN, etc.

- Approach 3: Integrate either variety with non-deep learning classifier, e.g., AE+SVM, CNN+SVM, etc.

Most of the hybrid networks have focused on supervised learning and classification tasks.

2.1.6 Deep Transfer Learning (DTL)

DTL uses a previously learned model to solve a new task with minimum training. The knowledge gained while solving one problem is stored and then applied or reused to a different but related problem. As an example, learning from recognizing cars can be partially used to recognize trucks. It can also be used to improve the sampling efficiency of a reinforcement learning agent. It is very useful when a needed amount of labeled data is unavailable or training on available data is expensive. Recently it has been used in many fields like natural language processing, sentiment classification, visual recognition, speech recognition, spam filtering, etc.

It has a two-stage process of pre-training and fine-tuning. DTL can be classified as having four main approaches as follows:

i. It utilizes instances in source domain by appropriate weight.

ii. It maps instances from two domains into a new data space with better similarity.

iii. It reuses a part of the network pretrained in the source domain based on network.

iv. It uses adversarial approach to transfer features suitable for two domains.

The last approach has become quite popular recently as it combines GAN and DTL. DTL can be also classified into (i) inductive, (ii) transductive, and (iii) unsupervised depending on the source and target domains.

2.1.7 Multi-Instance Learning (MIL)

MIL is a type of weakly supervised learning in which the learner receives a set of labeled sets or 'bags,' each containing many instances. For example, in multi-instance binary classification, a 'negative-labeled bag' contains all negative instances. A 'positive-labeled bag' contains at least one positive instance. The learning process leads one to the underlying concept for correct labeling.

In the simple case of binary classification, a bag labeled negative has all the negative instances, but one labeled positive has at least one positive instance. The learner uses a collection of such bags to either (i) induce a concept that will label individual instances correctly or (ii) learn how to label bags without inducing the concept. MIL is a kind of supervised learning, in which every training instance has either discrete or real valued label. It handles situations when training labels come with incomplete knowledge of labels.

2.2 LEARNING FROM STATISTICAL INFERENCE

Most of the learning methods discussed earlier can also be understood from a statistical point of view.

2.2.1 Inductive Inference

It is the same as supervised learning in which general rules are obtained from the labeled training data. The trained model is then used to predict the classification/regression properties of new and unseen data. In general, inductive learning first studies observation from which conclusions are drawn.

2.2.2 Deductive Inference

In general, deductive learning starts from the known conclusions or rules which helps the algorithms to classify the new observations.

2.2.3 Transductive Inference

Transductive learning (introduced by Vladimir Vapnik) was motivated by the observation that it is easier to learn a *specific* function for the specific problem at hand than a *general* function applicable to the same problem. Sometimes, it is preferable to induction as that requires solving a more general and often difficult problem. In those situations, many times it is easier to get the immediate solution without solving the general one. Transductive support vector machine (T-SVM) algorithm is an example of such an approach.

2.3 LEARNING DEPENDING ON TECHNIQUES

This way of looking at ML focusses on learning techniques. Some important variations are presented next.

2.3.1 Multitask Learning (MTL)

In MTL, multiple learning tasks are solved at the same time by exploiting features, which are both common and separate across tasks. This improves efficiency in learning and accuracy of prediction for the task-specific models when compared to situation when the models are trained separately. Usually, MTL is applied to stationary learning settings and its extension to nonstationary environments is called Group Online Adaptive Learning.

As MTL uses commonalities and differences across many tasks, to solve them at the same time, this leads to improved learning efficiency and prediction accuracy. It utilizes inductive transfer to improve generalization by using the domain information contained in the training signals of related tasks. Learning tasks is done in parallel, so learning each task helps better learn other tasks. Some good examples are spam filter, multi-class and multi-label classifications, etc. MTL is particularly useful when the tasks have many common features but are undersampled.

2.3.2 Active Learning (AL)

In AL, a learning algorithm queries a user (or some other information source also called *teacher* or *oracle*) to label new data points with the desired outputs, especially when unlabeled data is abundant but manual labeling is expensive. With careful choice the number of examples to learn a concept is often much lower than the number required in normal supervised learning.

2.3.3 Online Learning (OL)

In OL, data becomes available sequentially and is used to update the best predictor for future data at each step. This is different from batch learning for generating the best predictor by learning on the entire training data set at once.

2.3.4 Ensemble Learning (EL)

EL uses many learning algorithms to obtain performance that is better than any of the constituent learning algorithms alone. One can increase the resources to improve the efficiency of a single algorithm or spread that increase among multiple algorithms. The latter has been found to give better results.

An ML ensemble consisting of finite set of alternative models typically has more flexible alternative structures. In general, EL combines many hypotheses to construct a better hypothesis.

EL trains two or more algorithms to a specific classification or regression task, and they are called 'base models,' 'base learners' or 'weak learners.' A diverse collection of weak performing models are trained to the same modeling task, and as a result, their outcomes and error values exhibit high variance. Then EL combines them into a stronger and better performing model.

Ensemble learning uses Bagging (bootstrap-aggregating), Boosting, or Stacking/Blending techniques to create high variability base models.

- Bagging generates random samples from the training observations and tries fitting the same model to each different sample.

- Boosting is an iterative process to sequentially train each next base model on the up-weighted errors of the previous base model's errors. This produces an additive model to reduce the final model errors.

- Stacking or Blending trains different base models (with diverse/high variability) independently and combines them into the ensemble model.

Common EL applications include Random Forests (extension of Baggin), Boosted Tree Models, Gradient Boosted Tree Models.

In one sense, EL compensates for poor learning algorithms by performing a lot of extra computation. Fast algorithms such as decision trees and random forests are commonly used for this purpose.

2.4 REINFORCEMENT LEARNING (RL)

The foundation of RL has its origin in two scientific ideas of almost a century earlier.

1. Law of Effect
It was coined by Edward Thorndike in 1911 based on animal research. It is the notion that an animal will repeat satisfactory

actions and avoid actions producing discomfort. Furthermore, this says that the learning uses selection to choose the final course of action after observing how the possible choices worked. The animal also uses 'associative learning' in which options are associated with positive or negative outcomes.

In 1927, Ivan Pavlov described **reinforcement** as 'the strengthening of a pattern of behavior due to an animal receiving a stimulus—a reinforcer—in a time-dependent relationship with another stimulus or with a response.'

2. Optimal Control Theory

This has its origin in mathematics and algorithms. Richard Bellman used them to derive an equation (aptly named Bellman equation), which returns an optimal value function from given states of a dynamic system. He further introduced the idea of Markov decision process (MDP), which is a discrete stochastic version of the optimal control problem.

With the advent of NN, the RL was combined with it and deep RL (DRL) was born. In DRL, the agent learns from a high-dimensional environment using an NN which can be of two kinds.

i. Online or direct learning: The agent constructs an explicit model of the fully available environment and then computes an optimal policy for it.

ii. Offline or indirect learning: Full environment model is unavailable, so the agent uses one of the two options:

- It uses genetic algorithms, policy gradient methods, etc., to search the policy space, or

- It finds policy using value-learning methods (e.g., temporal difference, Q-learning, etc.) with either policy (like A2C, etc.) or value iteration schemes (e.g., Q-learning, etc.).

In both RL and DRL, the agent is given a task to perform or a goal to achieve. The overall system has many states and in each state an agent can take many possible actions. The agent chooses the action which maximizes the 'reward.'

   i. In RL, the agent accomplishes this task by trial and error. The reward is presented in a table so it can get that information in a straightforward manner. It is possible for the table to become too complex and many times the agent is unable to visit some state-action pairs.

   ii. In DRL, the agent uses NN to first learn the best possible state–action combination from an existing data set. It utilizes that knowledge to a new data set or a situation. The NN creates a function approximation for the reward implicitly, which the agent can use even for unencountered situations.

In coming chapters, we will discuss RL/DRL in more detail.

CHAPTER 3

Basic Mathematics behind Deep Reinforcement Learning

THE ORIGINS OF REINFORCEMENT learning (RL) lie in applied mathematics and statistics. There are many important concepts to understand that are essential for mastering both the theoretical and applied aspects of RL. This chapter focusses on them.

3.1 A MATHEMATICAL MODEL OF DRL

RL differs from other learning paradigms like unsupervised learning, supervised learning, etc., in some important ways, as given below.

- There is no supervision in RL so that there is no one telling the agent what the next best action is to be taken. For example, there is no supervisor guiding the robot in choosing the next moves.

DOI: 10.1201/9781032659800-3

- The feedback to the action taken is delayed and may not be observed immediately. This is very important as immediate action without feedback may lead to accidents.
- The agent decisions are sequential in time.
- The feedback to the agent depends on the actions taken by the agent and the uncertainty in the environment.

The RL has some important mathematical underpinnings:

- Markov decision process
- Bellman equations
- Q-learning

The rest of the chapter will explain these concepts.

3.2 MATHEMATICAL IDEAS BEHIND DRL

3.2.1 Markov Decision Process (MDP)

The MDP used in RL involves the elements $(S, A, P, r, \gamma, s_0)$ with the following properties:

- $\{S\}$ = the set of all states s, it may be finite or infinite
- $\{A\}$ = the set of all actions a, it may be finite or infinite
- $\{P\}$ = probability $P(s_{t+1} \mid s_t, a_t)$ for transitioning to state s_{t+1} at the next time step, after choosing action a_t in state s_t at time t.
- r = reward function $r(s_t, a_t)$ for choosing action a_t in state s_t, can be either deterministic or stochastic.
- γ = the discount factor to avoid accumulation of infinite future reward, so $\gamma < 1$.
- s_0 = the initial state which is usually taken from a distribution function.

MDP is a discounted process with infinite horizon. The *Markov property* is defined as follows:

> *The effect of an action (a) on a state (s) depends only on that state (s) and not on any prior history of its development.*

It means that no historical memory or the past information influences the next state. This makes the reasoning about the future states possible using only the information available in the current state. This is the basic mathematical framework behind the RL.

Let us look at these elements of MDP.

3.2.1.1 Actions and Policies

A policy defines how an agent selects actions. They can be either of the following depending on time horizon.

- *Stationary*:

  It applies for infinite time horizons, and stationary policies.

- *Nonstationary*:

  It depends on the time step and is useful for the finite time horizon. There, the cumulative rewards that the agent seeks to optimize are limited to a finite number of future time steps.

There is a second criterion for the policies which specifies the probability of the agent taking an action a_t in each state s_t. Let the parameters θ specify other dependencies of the policy, then it can have the following characteristics.

- *Deterministic*: In this case the probability is a predetermined time-independent action a.

$$\pi_\theta\left(s_t,a_t\right)=\pi_\theta\left(s\right)=a \qquad (3.1)$$

- *Stochastic*: Also, time-dependent in which case it is the probability of action a_t in state s_t

$$\pi_\theta\left(s_t,a_t\right)=P\left[a_t|s_t\right] \qquad (3.2)$$

Further, an RL agent can be either of the following kinds.

i. *Model-free*:

This agent has one or more of the following components:

- a *value function* predicting how good each state, or each state/action pair is, and
- a direct representation of the policy

The agent learns a policy π(a|s) without explicitly modeling the forward dynamics. It optimizes the policy by maximizing returns through estimation of policy gradients. For discrete situations Q-function is learned and for continuous cases both a value estimate and a policy is learned.

ii. *Model-based*:

This agent includes a model of the environment (estimated transition and reward functions) and a planning algorithm. The NN-based supervised learning is used to estimate a model of the environment. The actions are then learned by model predictive control using this model.

iii. *Mixed agent*:

This combines both approaches. For most real-world problems, the state space is high-dimensional and possibly continuous as well. In such situations deep learning

NN methods can be used to learn either policy or the value function.

- NN can deal with high-dimensional data, e.g., times series, frames, etc. They can manage exponential increase in data when adding extra dimensions to the state or action space.
- NN can be trained incrementally using additional samples obtained as learning happens.

3.2.1.2 Reward Function $r(s_t, a_t)$

It is a continuous scalar function in range $\{0, r_{max}\}$ for a given state-action pair to transition to another state. It indicates the quality of that state so that it is greater for states more relevant to the solution of the task. Rewards are defined by the following terms.

- *Rewards*:
  They are associated with single states and indicate the states' quality.
- *Return*:
  This indicates the quality of full sequence of decisions made in reaching the goal. The reward for such a full sequence is called *return*.
- *Value function*:
  It is the expected cumulative reward when actions are taken according to a policy.

Later in this chapter we discuss the varieties of value functions.

3.2.1.3 Discount Factor

The tasks can be of two kinds and that will affect their nature.

- *Continuous time* and *long running tasks*

In these tasks it makes sense to discount far-future rewards to value current information more strongly at the present time.

To achieve this the discount factor $\gamma<1$ such that the impact of faraway rewards is reduced. In this way, the cumulative reward does not become infinite, and the agent can reach its reward goal in finite time.

- Episodic tasks
These tasks come to an end, and discounting factor considerations do not apply. So, in these problems, $\gamma = 1$ is used.

3.3 VALUE AND POLICY FUNCTIONS

In addition to the sets of states and functions we also need various value functions which are related to rewards. They depend on the process parameters for controlling the behavior of the RL agent involving states, actions, or their combinations. Some commonly used value functions are described next.

3.3.1 State-Only Value Function $v_\pi(s)$

It is the expected return or reward (denoted by r_t) starting from that state under the agent's policy π_θ.

$$v_\pi(s) = E_\pi\left[\sum_{k=0}^{\infty}\gamma^k r_{k+t+1} \mid s_t = s\right] \qquad (3.3)$$

The discount factor $(\gamma<1)$ ensures the finiteness of the accumulated reward.

Expression for value function in terms of policy

3.3.2 State-Action Value Function $Q^\pi(s, a)$

This is also known simply as Q-function where Q denotes quality). If the agent's policy π_θ is given, then it is the expected return or reward starting from that state, taking that action.

$$Q^\pi(s,a) = E_\pi\left[\sum_{k=0}^{\infty}\gamma^k r_{k+t+1} \mid s_t = s, a_t = a\right] \qquad (3.4)$$

Here

- $Q^{\pi}(s,a)$ = the expected total future reward (under policy π with discount factor γ) at time t for a given state-action pair (s_t, a_t).
- r_{t+1} = the reward at time step $t+1$ and so on.

The right-hand side in the above equation is an expectation value (denoted by E) as the expression inside the bracket is a random variable.

3.3.3 Action-Only Value Function $V^{\pi}(a_t)$

It is the value of an action a_t at time t under policy π over all the states. It is also denoted just as V-function.

$$V^{\pi}(a_t) = \sum_{s_t} Q^{\pi}(s_t, a_t) \pi_{\theta}(s_t, a_t) \qquad (3.5)$$

3.3.4 Advantage Value Function $A^{\pi}(s_t, a_t)$

It is the difference between the *Q-function* and *V-function*, and it considers the other actions that the agent could have taken.

$$A^{\pi}(s_t, a_t) = Q^{\pi}(s_t, a_t) - V^{\pi}(a_t) \qquad (3.6)$$

3.3.5 Policy Function with Maximum Entropy π^*_{maxEnt}

The previously defined Q-function does not prioritize the more promising states to be visited by the agent. One way to implement this idea is to define the policy directly in terms of exponentiated Q-values.

$$\pi_{\theta}(s_t, a_t) \propto \exp Q^{\pi}(s_t, a_t) \qquad (3.7)$$

Here the Q-function serves as the negative energy in a Boltzmann-like distribution, and it assigns a nonzero likelihood to all actions. Because of this, the agent becomes aware of all behaviors that lead to solving the task. This can help the agent adapt to changing situations in which some of the solutions might have become infeasible.

The policy defined now is an optimal solution for the maximum-entropy RL objective.

$$\pi^*_{\text{MaxEnt}} = \text{argmax}_\pi E_\pi \left[\sum_{t=0}^{T} r_t + H(\pi(.\,|\,s_t)) \right] \quad (3.8)$$

Here H is the entropy function.

3.4 BELLMAN EQUATIONS (BE)

The value functions follow the Bellman equations named after their discoverer Richard E. Bellman (1949). The basic idea behind most of them is the following observation.

Define the cumulative discounted reward function as

$$R_t(\gamma,T) = \sum_{k=t+1}^{T} \gamma^{k-(t+1)} r_k = r_{t+1} + \gamma r_{t+2} + \gamma^2 r_{t+3} \dots + \gamma^{T-(t+1)} r_T$$

$$= r_{t+1} + \gamma\left(r_{t+2} + \gamma r_{t+3} + +\gamma^2 r_{t+4} \dots + \gamma^{T-(t+2)} r_T\right) \quad (3.9)$$

Here the final time T can be infinity and γ can be 1 (but not both at the same time). One can write the above as a recursive relation.

$$R_t(\gamma,T) = r_{t+1} + \gamma R_{t+1}(\gamma,T) \quad (3.10)$$

3.4.1 BE for the State Value Function $V_\pi(s)$
It has the following definition.

$$v_\pi(s) = E_\pi\left[R_t(\gamma,T)|s_t = s\right] \quad (3.11)$$

The earlier expression for $R_t(\gamma,T)$ gives

$$v_\pi(s) = E_\pi\left[r_{t+1}\right] + \gamma E_\pi\left[R_{t+1}(\gamma,T)|s_t = s\right] \quad (3.12)$$

Finally, using the definition of $v_\pi(s)$ leads to the desired BE.

$$v_\pi(s) = E_\pi\left[r_{t+1} + \gamma v_\pi(s_{t+1})|s_t = s\right] \quad (3.13)$$

Without the expectation value operation, it takes the following equivalent form:

$$v_\pi(s_t) = r_t + \sum_{s_{t+1}}\gamma P(s_{t+1}|s_t,a_t)v_\pi(s_{t+1}) \quad (3.14)$$

Note that the first term is different. Then the optimized value in the current state is

$$v_\pi^*(s_t) = r_t + \max_{a_t}\sum_{s_{t+1}}\gamma P(s_{t+1}|s_t,a_t)v_\pi(s_{t+1}) \quad (3.15)$$

This gives the optimal policy for choosing the next action, which maximizes the future reward.

$$\pi^*(s_t) = \arg\max_{a_t}\sum_{s_{t+1}}P(s_{t+1}|s_t,a_t)v_\pi^*(s_t) \quad (3.16)$$

3.4.2 BE for the State-Action Value Function $Q^\pi(s,a)$
It is given as follows:

$$Q_\pi^*(s,a) = E_\pi\left[R_t(\gamma,T)|s_t = s,a_t = a\right]$$
$$= E_\pi\left[r_{t+1} + \gamma R_{t+1}(\gamma,T)|s_t = s,s_t = s,a_t = a\right]$$
$$= E_\pi\left[r_{t+1} + \gamma Q^\pi(s_{t+1},a_{t+1})|s_t = s,a_t = a\right] \quad (3.17)$$

Optimal control policy produces optimal value functions.

$$Q_\pi^*\left(s_t,a_t\right)=r_{t+1}+\max_{a_t}\sum_{s_{t+1},a_{t+1}}\gamma P(s_{t+1}\mid s_t,a_t)Q_\pi\left(s_{t+1},a_{t+1}\right) \quad (3.18)$$

3.4.3 Soft BE for the Value Function of a State

It is like the previous ones but uses a special function called **softmax** in the expectation value.

$$Q\left(s_t,a_t\right)=E\left[r_t+\gamma*softmax_a\ Q\left(s_t,a\right)\right] \quad (3.19)$$

Here the **softmax** function is defined as

$$softmax_a f\left(a\right)=\log\int\exp f\left(a\right)da \quad (3.20)$$

The soft BE holds for the optimal Q-function of the entropy augmented reward function. The soft BE allows solving for the Q-function using dynamic programming or model-free temporal difference (TD) learning in tabular state and action spaces.

Some analytical solutions for Bellman equation are given in the Appendix.

3.5 LOSS FUNCTIONS

The loss and cost are very important factors for meeting the NN goals as they measure how good the ML algorithm models the input data set in predicting the expected outcome. Generally, it is defined as the difference between the mean squared error of the predicted Q-value from the target Q-value Q*. In this context, **loss function** (LF) is calculated for each sample and the **cost function** is its average for all samples. They need to be minimized to improve the performance of the algorithm.

LF for classification predicts the probabilities of all the classes inherent in the input data. Some important ones are described below. Similarly, LF for regression applies to situations with continuous variables.

3.5.1 LF for Classification: Binary Cross-Entropy Loss/Log Loss

This is one of the most used loss functions in classification. It measures the performance of a classification model whose predicted output is a probability value between 0 and 1. It decreases as the predicted probability converges to the actual label.

$$L = -\frac{1}{m}\sum_{i=1}^{m}\left[y_i \log \hat{y}_i + \left(1 - y_i\right)\log\left(1 - \hat{y}_i\right)\right] \quad (3.21)$$

where

- m = the number of training samples,
- i = the ith training sample,
- y_i = value of the ith sample, and
- $\hat{y}_i$ = value of the predicted ith sample.

It is called *binary classification* for two classes and *multi-class classification* for more than two classes.

3.5.2 LF for Classification: Hinge Loss

This loss function is highly used in support vector machine (SVM) model evaluation.

$$L = \max\left(0, 1 - yf\left(x\right)\right) \quad (3.22)$$

where y is the sample value and $f\left(x\right)$ is the SVM value.

It penalizes the wrong predictions and the right predictions that are not confident. For SVM classifiers it uses class labels -1 and 1.

Loss functions for regression are used for problems with continuous inputs. Some important ones are given below.

3.5.3 LF for Regression: Mean Square Error (MSE)/Quadratic Loss/L2 Loss

We define MSE loss function as the average of squared differences between the actual and the predicted value. It is the most used regression loss function.

$$MSE = \frac{1}{n}\sum_{i=1}^{n}\left(\hat{Y}_i - Y_i\right)^2 \qquad (3.23)$$

where n is the number of training samples, i is the ith training sample, and $Y_i/\hat{Y}_i$ is the value of the ith sample and its predicted value. *The MSE penalizes the large errors by squaring them, which makes it less robust to outliers.*

3.5.4 LF for Regression: Mean Absolute Error (MAE)/L1 Loss

The MAE is the average of absolute differences between the actual and the predicted values. It measures the average magnitude of errors in a set of predictions without considering their directions.

$$MAE = \frac{1}{n}\sum_{i=1}^{n}\left|y_i - x_i\right| \qquad (3.24)$$

where x_i/y_i is the actual/predicted value and n is the number of samples. **It is more robust to outliers compared to the MSE and therefore it is preferred if** the data is prone to many outliers.

3.5.5 LF for Regression: Huber Loss/Smooth Mean Absolute Error

It combines MSE and MAE. It is MAE and becomes quadratic for small error. That is controlled by a tunable hyperparameter δ.

$$L_\delta\left(y, f\left(x\right)\right) = \frac{1}{2}\left(y - f\left(x\right)\right)^2, \text{for } \left|y - f\left(x\right)\right| \le \delta$$

$$= \delta\left|y - f\left(x\right)\right| - \frac{1}{2}\delta^2, \text{ otherwise} \qquad (3.25)$$

where y is the actual value and $f\left(x\right)$ is the predicted value. The choice of δ is critical as it determines what an outlier is. This loss function should be preferred for the outlier-prone data.

3.5.6 LF for Regression: Log-Cosh Loss

It is the logarithm of the hyperbolic cosine of the prediction error and is much smoother than MSE. It is twice differentiable everywhere, and used for some learning algorithms like XGBoost which uses Newton's method to find the optimum.

$$L\left(y, y^p\right) = \sum_{i=1}^{n} log(cosh(y_i^p - y_i))$$
$$\approx x^2 / 2 \text{ for small } x, |x| - log\,(2)\text{ for large } x$$
$$(3.26)$$

Here $y_i^p - y_i$ is the predicted error or x. It is mostly like the MSE but is not affected strongly by the occasional incorrect prediction.

3.5.7 LF for Regression: Quantile Loss

The quantile regression loss function predicts quantiles, which are values below which a fraction of samples in a group falls. For a set of predictions, the loss will be its average.

$$L_\gamma\left(y, y^p\right) = \sum_{i=y_i < y_i^p} \left(\gamma - 1\right)\left|y_i - y_i^p\right| + \sum_{i=y_i \ge y_i^p} \gamma\left|y_i - y_i^p\right| \quad (3.27)$$

where $y_i^p - y_i$ is the predicted error and γ is the hyperparameter. It is useful for predicting an interval instead of only points.

There are many loss functions specific to the ML tasks like object and face recognition. They are in most cases special cases based on the general ideas.

3.6 ACTIVATION FUNCTIONS

The activation functions are used at the internal NN layers to bring the quantity of interest within (0, 1) interval.

3.6.1 Activation Functions: Sigmoid

It is a mathematical function with a characteristic 'S'-shaped curve – hence the name sigmoid. In the area of AI/ML, it is usually another name for the logistic function defined below for a single variable.

$$\sigma(x) = \frac{1}{1+e^{-x}} = 1 - \sigma(-x) \qquad (3.28)$$

A sigmoid function is convex for values less than a particular point, and it is concave for values greater than that point. There is also one inflection point. When used in the NNs, they show some problems as well.

- Vanishing gradients for very high or very low values.
- Output not centered on 0 which reduces the efficiency of weight update.
- Exponential operations are slow for computers.

Some other common sigmoid functions are given below.

- Hyperbolic tangent function

$$\sigma(x) = \tanh(x) = \frac{2}{1+e^{-2x}} - 1 \qquad (3.29)$$

It has some advantages compared with sigmoid.

- Output interval is 1 and it is centered on 0.
- Negative input is mapped to negative and zero input is mapped to near-zero.

In binary classification problem, tanh is used for the **hidden layer** and the sigmoid is used for the **output layer in general**.

- Arctangent function

$$\sigma(x) = \arctan(x) \qquad (3.30)$$

- Gudermannian function

$$\sigma(x) = 2\arctan\left(\tanh\left(\frac{x}{2}\right)\right) \qquad (3.31)$$

3.6.2 Activation Functions: Softmax

It takes a vector **z** of K real numbers as input and brings out a probability distribution as output.

$$\sigma(z)_i = \frac{e^{z_i}}{\sum_{j=1}^{K} e^{z_j}}, i = 1, 2, \ldots, K \qquad (3.32)$$

The vector input components can be negative or greater than 1. The output of the softmax function lies in the interval $(0,1)$ with all components adding up to 1. The larger components yield larger probabilities. The softmax function is actually the well-known Boltzmann probability function of statistical thermodynamics adapted to ML.

3.6.3 Activation Functions: Rectified Linear Unit (ReLU)

ReLU is a very popular activation function and is defined as follows.

$$\sigma(x) = \max(0, x), \ x \geq 0 \ and \ 0 \ for \ x < 0 \qquad (3.33)$$

It is 0 for x less than 0 and x for x greater than or equal to x. It has the range $[0, \infty]$. ReLU has no gradient saturation problem for positive x and is computed much faster compared to sigmoid and tanh. On the other hand, it has also some disadvantages.

- For negative x, it is completely inactive. This is problematic for backpropagation.
- It is not centered on 0.

There are variations of ReLU which take care of its shortcomings. Leaky ReLU (LReLU) is defined as

$$\sigma(x) = x, x > 0 \ and \ ax \ for \ x \leq 0 \qquad (3.34)$$

It gives a very small value to negative inputs using small 'a,' *e.g., a = 0.01. Range is also increased to* $[-\infty, \infty]$. It also solves the problem of dead ReLU.

- Exponential linear unit (ELU) is defined as

$$\sigma(x) = x, x > 0 \ and \ a(e^x - 1) \ for \ x \leq 0. \qquad (3.35)$$

Its negative values bring the mean closer to zero, so it is zero-centered, and the gradients are also closer to their natural values. Learning is faster due to a reduced bias shift effect. Even smaller inputs saturate ELUs to negative values, thus decreasing the variations in forward propagation. It is slightly more computationally intensive compared to ReLU.

- Parametric ReLU (PReLU) is defined as

$$\sigma(x) = x, \; x > 0 \; and \; ax \; for \; x \le 0 \,. \tag{3.36}$$

It is a generalization of ReLU such that other versions are its special cases, e.g.,

- **a** = 0 makes it ReLU,
- **a** > 0 makes it LReLU, and for
- **a** as a learnable parameter it is PReLU.

  It has a small nonzero slope in the **x** ≤ 0 region so the problem of ReLU death is avoided.

In actual applications no clear-cut and definitive advantage has been found between the original ReLU and its variations.

3.7 ENTROPIES AND RELATED FUNCTIONS

The systems of both natural and human-made varieties are built out of many smaller or less complex entities, e.g., gas made up of molecules or atoms. Such systems have disorder or chaos as their inherent property, and it is mathematically captured by the idea of entropy.

The concept was later applied by Shannon to information. It has many variations as there are many ways in which the randomness inherent in such systems can be captured. Here we give a list of entropies with their definitions.

3.7.1 Boltzmann's Thermodynamic Entropy

It is the starting point of many similar definitions of entropy. For an isolated state in thermodynamic equilibrium, it is defined as

$$S = -k_B ln\Omega \tag{3.37}$$

where k_B is Boltzmann's constant, ln is the natural logarithm, and Ω is the number of microstates with energy same as the system's energy. The Boltzmann entropy can be further generalized as

$$S = -k_B Tr\left(\hat{\rho}\ln\hat{\rho}\right) \tag{3.38}$$

where $\hat{\rho}$ is the density matrix, Tr is the trace, and ln is the natural matrix logarithm. All other definitions of entropy can be derived from it.

3.7.2 Gibbs Entropy
It is defined as

$$S = -k_B \sum_i p_i \ln p_i \tag{3.39}$$

It is the generalization of the Boltzmann entropy. The latter refers to the situation when the system is in a global thermodynamic equilibrium. The former does not require the system to be in a single state. It is also referred to as Boltzmann–Gibbs entropy.

3.7.3 Tsallis Entropy
It is a further generalization of Boltzmann–Gibbs entropy for nonadditive and nonstandard thermodynamic situations. Let $\{p_i\}$ be the discrete set of probabilities ($\sum_i p_i = 1$), real number q be the entropic index, and k be a positive number, then Tsallis entropy is defined by

$$S_q(P) = \frac{k}{q-1}\left(1 - \sum_i p_i^q\right) \tag{3.40}$$

The usual Botzmann–Gibbs entropy is recovered in the limit $q \to 1$.

3.7.4 Rényi Entropy

It is named after Alfred Rényi who generalized the concept of information while preserving the additivity of independent events. It is defined as

$$H_\alpha(P) = \frac{1}{1-\alpha} log\left(\sum_{i=1}^{n} p_i^\alpha\right) \qquad (3.41)$$

Here $0 < \alpha < \infty$, $\alpha \neq 1$, and p_i is the probability for random variable with $i=1,...,n$. Many other information-theoretic entropies, e.g., Hartley entropy, Shannon entropy, collision entropy, and min-entropy, are special cases of Rényi entropy. In many physics-based models it is essentially the trace of the power of the density matrix.

$$H_\alpha(P) = \frac{1}{1-\alpha} log\left(Tr\rho^\alpha\right) \qquad (3.42)$$

The exact analytic expression for Rényi entropy of Heisenberg XY spin model is known.

3.7.5 Shannon or Information Entropy

The basic idea of entropy in physics was modified and applied to information theory by Shannon by developing the concept of information entropy. This gives the average number of bits so that the information can be stored optimally. For information of n symbols, the average number of bits must be at the least $log_2 n$. This idea is captured by the information entropy H defined by

$$\text{Discrete case: } H = -\sum_{i=1}^{n} p_i log_2 p_i \qquad (3.43)$$

where p_i is the probability of an outcome from the set of all possibilities. It has some interesting properties: (i) S increases to a maximum value of $log_2 n$ when all p_i are equal to $1/n$, and (ii) for only one possible outcome the system is perfectly predictable, and so $H = 0$.

For continuous probability distribution it is given as

$$\text{Continuous case: } H(P) = -\sum_x P(x)\log P(x) \quad (3.44)$$

3.7.6 Hartley Entropy

Given a finite set with n elements, if we choose an element randomly, then the information obtained is expressed by Hartley function, also known as Hartley entropy or max-entropy.

$$H(P) = \log_2 n \quad (3.45)$$

3.7.7 Collision Entropy

It is a special case of Rényi entropy when $\alpha = 2$.

$$H_2(P) = -log\left(\sum_{i=1}^n p_i^2\right) = -log|\boldsymbol{p}|^2 \quad (3.46)$$

Here $|p| = \sqrt{\sum_{i=1}^n p_i^2}$ is the geometric length of an n-dimensional vector.

3.7.8 Min-Entropy

In the limit $\alpha \to \infty$, Rényi entropy is called min-entropy.

$$H_\infty(P) = -\log max_i p_i \quad (3.47)$$

It is the smallest entropy measure in the family of Rényi entropies – hence its name. It is never larger than Shannon's entropy.

3.7.9 Cross-Entropy

This is a generalization of Shannon's entropy to two probability distribution $P(x)$ and $Q(x)$ over the same support space.

$$H(P,Q) = -\sum_x P(x)\log Q(x) \qquad (3.48)$$

As an example, cross-entropy is minimized between the data distribution and the model distribution for maximum likelihood estimation in supervised learning.

3.7.10 Relative Entropy or Kullback–Leibler (KL) Divergence

It is the expectation value of logarithmic difference between two probability distribution. For discrete probability distributions (P = 'true' and Q = given probability distribution), it is

$$D_{KL}(P||Q) = \sum_x P(x)\log\left(\frac{P(x)}{Q(x)}\right) = -\sum_x P(x)\log\left(\frac{Q(x)}{P(x)}\right)$$

$$(3.49)$$

The KL divergence and cross-entropy are related as

$$H(P,Q) = H(P) + D_{KL}(P||Q) \qquad (3.50)$$

There are many more definitions of entropy relevant to other branches of mathematics, e.g., Kolmogorov–Sinai entropy, topological entropy, metric entropy, etc.

3.7.11 Mutual Information

It is a measure of the mutual dependence between two variables defined as the amount of information obtained about one random variable by observing the other. It determines how different the joint distribution of pair (X, Y) is from the product of their marginal distributions. It is defined in terms of KL divergence as

$$I(X,Y) = D_{KL}(P_{(X,Y)} || P_X \oplus P_Y) \qquad (3.51)$$

Broadly speaking, it quantifies the information shared by two distributions.

3.7.12 Information Gain

It is the amount of information gained about a random signal or variable X from observing another one Y. It is basically the KL divergence defined earlier and is another name for the same. In the context of decision trees, it is the same as mutual information.

3.7.13 Fisher Information

Many times, one needs the amount of information carried by an unknown parameter θ of a distribution which models a random observable X. This is given by Fisher information $I(\theta)$, which depends on covariances.

$$I(\theta) = E\left[\left(\frac{\partial}{\partial\theta}\log f(X;\theta)\right)^2 \Big| \theta\right] = \int\left(\frac{\partial}{\partial\theta}\log f(X,\theta)\right)^2 f(x;\theta)dx$$

$$(3.52)$$

In an equivalent manner, it gives an estimate of the relative uncertainty in and correlation among the model parameters based on the local curvature of the cost function.

APPENDIX: SOME ANALYTICAL SOLUTIONS OF BELLMAN EQUATION

The BE equations are solved using methods of dynamic programming. The term 'programming' here refers to the original meaning of this term introduced by Bellman. It uses recursive methods to calculate the value of a state by calling on its own code to complete recursive steps. This approach in its simple application goes through the entire state space many times. This inefficiency is addressed by better methods that were developed afterward.

There are very few known analytically solvable models for BE. The following examples present a few of them.

i. Model – 1

This example is from the area of econometrics.

Input

s_t = state variable,

Bellman equation: $V(s_t) = max_{s_{t+1}} \left[u(s_t^\theta - s_{t+1}) + \gamma V(s_{t+1}) \right]$

$$\text{Where } u(c_t) = \log(c_t) \qquad (3.53)$$

Solution:

Let

$V_t(s_t)$ be the value function when there are t periods left to go, $V_0(s_t) = 0$

The policy rule: $\alpha_t(s_t) = s_{t+1}$ with $\alpha_0(k_t) = 0$

Then

$$V_1(s_t) = \log(s_t^k) = k \log(s_t) \qquad (3.54)$$

$$V_2(s_t) = max_{s_{t+1}} \left[\log(s_t^k - s_{t+1}) + \gamma V_1(s_{t+1}) \right]$$

$$= max_{s_{t+1}} \left[\log(s_t^k - s_{t+1}) + \gamma k \log(s_{t+1}) \right] \qquad (3.55)$$

Maximization gives

$$\frac{d}{ds_{t+1}} V_2(s_t) = \frac{d}{ds_{t+1}} \left[\log(s_t^k - s_{t+1}) + \gamma k \log(s_{t+1}) \right] = 0 \qquad (3.56)$$

So that

$$s_{t+1} = \frac{\gamma k}{1 + \gamma k} s_t^k \qquad (3.57)$$

Substitution leads to

$$V_2(s_t) = k(1 + \gamma k)\log(s_t) + D \qquad (3.58)$$

The last term is time independent.

$$D = \gamma k \log(\gamma k) - (1 + \gamma k)\log(1 + \gamma k) \qquad (3.59)$$

Iterating the steps n times gives

$$V_n(s_t) = k(1 + \gamma k + \gamma^2 k^2 + \ldots + \gamma^{n-1} k^{n-1})\log(s_t) + \gamma D \qquad (3.60)$$

As $n \to \infty$, we get a solution to BE.

$$V(s_t) = \frac{k}{1 - \gamma k}\log(s_t) + \gamma\left[\gamma k \log(\gamma k) - (1 + \gamma k)\log(1 + \gamma k)\right] \qquad (3.61)$$

ii. Model – 2

The following continuous example is from quantum control theory.

Let V^* be the optimal value function satisfying the following Bellman equation.

$$-\partial_t V^* = \min_{B_t}\left\{B_t^2 + 2B_t\partial_\theta V^*\right\} + 2\alpha^2\partial_{\theta\theta}^2 V^* \qquad (3.62)$$

Completing the squares gives the optimal condition.

$$B_t = -\partial_\theta V^* \qquad (3.63)$$

Substitution in the starting BE leads to Hamilton–Jacobi–Bellman equation.

$$\partial_t V^* = \left(\partial_\theta V^*\right)^2 - 2\alpha^2 \partial^2_{\theta\vartheta} V^* \tag{3.64}$$

Let us make an ansatz: $V^*(t) = \theta_t^2 f(t) + g(t)$. Then the substitution gives the equations for the unknown functions as

$$\partial_t f = 4f^2, f(T) = 1 \tag{3.65}$$

$$\partial_t g = -4\alpha^2 f, g(T) = 0 \tag{3.66}$$

The solutions are

$$f(t) = \frac{1}{4(T-t)+1}, g(t) = \alpha^2 \log\left|4(T-t)+1\right| \tag{3.67}$$

$$V^*(t) = \frac{\theta_t^2}{4(T-t)+1} + \alpha^2 \log\left|4(T-t)+1\right| \tag{3.68}$$

CHAPTER 4

Single-Agent Algorithms

T HE HISTORICAL DEVELOPMENT OF RL started with the situations where the number of possible states and actions were finite and discrete. Usually, these could be presented in a tabular form. Many games of strategy like Go and Chess fall under this category. Neural networks are not needed for their solution, so they are not deep RL but simply RL algorithms.

There are many approaches to RL depending on which aspect is emphasized. This leads to many algorithms, some of which are very general, and others better suited to specific problems. We start with general considerations applicable to the classification of RL algorithms by understanding the applicable environment.

DOI: 10.1201/9781032659800-4

i. Deterministic versus stochastic

The reward for every (state, action) pair is known in a deterministic environment. In stochastic situation they are known probabilistically.

ii. Finite versus infinite horizon

The agent comes to a stop in the former but can go on operating indefinitely in the latter scenario.

iii. The environment is **static** and so it does not vary with time. Time-varying environments call for different approaches.

The algorithms have the following general characteristics.

i. **Algorithm:** The common name by which it is known is given.

ii. **Model:** The agent learns either from value or from policy rewards obtained by going through the (state, action) pairs. It can be also model free in which case all possibilities of model are given right at the beginning.

iii. **Action:** It can be either discrete or continuous.

iv. **Policy:** For a learned model, one may have either offline or online learning.

- *OFF Policy*: A replay buffer memory stores the previous states and randomly chooses a batch to train the model. It does not update the model based on the current performance.

- *ON Policy*: The model is updated at each episode based on the current exploration of the agent. It converges slowly and is a bit noisy because it uses an exploration only once.

v. **Performance measure:** The basic mathematical or statistical measure characterizing the performance of the algorithm is given.

The method of *temporal difference* (TD) learning has been a very important feature of model-free learning in which the role of the transition function is replaced by an iterative sequence of environment samples. The TD here refers to the difference in values between two time steps used to calculate the value at the new time step. It works by updating the current estimate of the state value with an error value based on the estimate of the state that it has gotten through sampling the environment:

$$V(s) \leftarrow V(s) + \alpha[r' + \gamma V(s') - V(s)] \qquad (4.1)$$

where s is the current state, s' is the new state, r is the reward of the new state, α is the learning rate, and γ is the discount rate. The learning rate α controls how fast the algorithm learns (or bootstraps), so setting its value too high can be detrimental since the last value dominates the bootstrap process too much. Its optimal value is found by experimentation. The last term subtracts the value of the current state to compute the TD. Another way to write this update rule is

$$V(s) \leftarrow \alpha[r' + \gamma V(s')] + (1 - \alpha)V(s) \qquad (4.2)$$

as the difference between the new TD target and the old value. Note the absence of transition model T in the formula; TD is a model-free update formula.

Almost all RL algorithms follow a generic framework and are typically a variant of the scheme given below. They try attacking one step or multiple steps of the problem.

- Loop:
  Collect trajectories ((transitions – (state, action, reward, next state, terminated flag)))
  (Optionally) Store trajectories in a replay buffer for sampling

- Loop:

  Sample a mini batch of transitions to compute policy gradient.

  (Optionally) Compute critic Gradient
- Update parameters

The single-agent discrete algorithms apply to situations where a finite number of actions and states for the agent. Some well-known algorithms are given in the table below. Simple value-iteration for discrete states is a simple approach based on dynamic programming for finding optimal state value-function. One solves a Bellman equation for Markov Decision Process (MDP) given by five elements:

i. **A set of states** representing all possible agent configurations in the environment,

ii. **A set of actions** the agent can take in any given state,

iii. **Transition probabilities** that the agent's action will be successful (or not),

iv. **Rewards**, for arriving to a specific state, and

v. **A discount factor γ** for diminishing future rewards.

One starts at time t with (i) an initial state s_t, (ii) the initial reward r_t, and (iii) discount factor $0 < \gamma \le 1$. The algorithm calculates the new value-function after looking at all possible actions available to the agent and maximizing the value.

$$v(s_t) = r_t + \gamma \max_{a_t}\left[\sum_{s_{t+1}} P(s_{t+1}|s_t, a_t) v(s_{t+1})\right], \forall s_t \quad (4.3)$$

The value of being in a state is a sum of

i. Immediate reward in that state, and

ii. The discount factor multiplied with the maximum value of the expression in the bracket found after calculating it over all actions allowed in that state.

The expression in the bracket for a chosen action itself is the value function of the possible transition state multiplied with transition probabilities of that state and it is summed over all reachable transition states.

i. Algorithms based on MDP: They are again broadly classified into the following.
- Model based:
  - Model is given: MCTS.
  - Model is learned: I2A, World model.
- Model free:
  - Value-based and on-policy: SARSA,
  - Value-based and off-policy: Q-learning, DQN.
  - Policy-based and gradient-free:
    a. Using cross-entropy: QT-opt,
    b. Using evolution strategy: SAMUEL.
  - Both policy- and gradient-based: Policy gradient, TRPO/PPO, ACKTR.

ii. Algorithms based on multi-arm-bandits paradigm.
- Action value-based.
- Gradient-based.

In the rest of the chapter some important but (nonexhaustive) algorithms are introduced.

4.1 Q-LEARNING

Algorithm	Model	Action	Policy	Perf. Meas.
Q-Learning	Model-free	Discrete	Discrete, off	Q-function

It is one of the early RL algorithms developed by Chris Watkins in 1989. In this approach, the learned Q-function at each iteration approximates the optimal value function for action. Given a state, it is a model-free RL algorithm for learning the value of an action. It finds an optimal policy so that expected total reward or Q-function over all successive steps is maximized. The Bellman equation is used for value iteration. The following steps illustrate the procedure.

The Q-learning is a *model-free* algorithm for learning the value of an action. The agent finds an optimal policy so that the '**Q-function**' (the expected total reward) over all successive steps is maximized. A SARSA agent uses an *on-policy learning* to interact with the environment and updates modifiable parameters after each visit of a state. The Monte Carlo methods rely on repeated random sampling to approximate situations which may be deterministic in principle.

In the *finite state-action Q-learning*, big memory space is needed for storage. That need makes its generalization to continuous state-action situation almost impossible. This problem is solved by approximating the Q-function using deep neural network called DQN. It computes the Q-values of all possible actions for a given input state. The size of its input and output layers is that of the states and all possible actions, respectively. The agent forwards its state to the DQN and chooses the action with the highest Q-value.

System Setup
Start at time t with an (i) initial state s_t, (ii) the initial reward r_t, (iii) the initial state-action value-function $Q(s_t, a_t)$, (iv) learning rate or step size α, and (v) discount factor $0 < \gamma \leq 1$.

Pseudocode
The algorithm uses a Bellman equation for updating a simple value function by calculating the weighted average of the current value and the new information.

At $t = 0$

assign a random value to $Q(s_t, a_t)$

At time t

(i) Choose an action a_t and calculate the new Q-function.

$$Q^{new}(s_t, a_t) = Q(s_t, a_t) +$$
$$\alpha\left[r_t + \gamma max_a Q(s_{t+1}, a) - Q(s_t, a_t)\right] \quad (4.4)$$

With

$Q(s_t, a_t)$ = old Q-function value,

r_t = reward,

$max_a Q(s_{t+1}, a)$ = future Q-function estimate (optimized for chosen action)

the terms in the Bellman equation above are:

- $(1 - \alpha)Q(s_t, a_t)$ = current Q-function weighted by learning rate
- ar_t = the reward (weighted by learning rate) obtained if action a_t is taken
- $\alpha\gamma\, max_a Q(s_t, a_t)$ = the maximum reward (weighted by learning rate and discount factor) that can be obtained if new state is s_{t+1}

(ii) Calculate $Q^{new}(s_t, a_t)$ for all other possible actions a_t and find its maximum value.

(iii) Choose the action corresponding to the maximum value.

(iv) Update the action corresponding to the maximum value.

Repeat the process for next time steps.

Stop when state s_{t+1} is terminal or final state (Q-function for this state can be zero)

Applications

The Q-learning has found applications in many areas, out of which some prominent ones are:

i. Autoconfiguration of online web systems,

ii. News recommendation system, and

iii. Network traffic control system.

4.2 DEEP Q-LEARNING AND DEEP Q-NETWORK (DQN)

Algorithm	Model	Action	Policy	Perf. Meas.
Deep Q-Learning	Model-free	Continuous	Continuous, off	Q-function

It is the generalization of the finite Q-learning presented before to continuous states and actions. They cannot be represented by a table for such situations as the potential combinations can become infinite. The solution of such systems requires neural networks (NN) and is indicated by the word 'Deep' in the Deep Q-learning or DQN. Policy gradient is a very important general tool for these algorithms. They solve the problem of 'reward shaping' or finding the right set of rewards for a given problem. This is done by a policy which is the probability distribution for a given state.

4.2.1 Mathematical Formulation

Let

- θ = the set of parameters defining a policy π, e.g., the coefficients of a polynomial or the weights and biases of neural network nodes
- τ = the trajectory (set of states and actions) of an agent resulting in the reward $r(\tau)$

Then the 'expected' reward following the policies parameterized by θ is given as

$$J(\theta) = E_{\pi}\left[r(\tau)\right] = \int \pi(\tau) r(\tau) d\tau \qquad (4.5)$$

Let θ^* denote parameter maximizing $J(\theta)$. That can be found by first calculating the gradient of $J(\theta)$,

$$\nabla J(\theta) = \nabla \int \pi(\tau) r(\tau) d\tau = E_\pi \big[r(\tau) \nabla \log \pi(\tau) \big] \quad (4.6)$$

and utilizing the gradient ascent rule for update as

$$\theta_{t+1} = \theta_t + \alpha \nabla J(\theta_t) \quad (4.7)$$

The Policy Gradient Theorem: We use the following obvious result:

Derivative of the expected reward = the expectation of the reward × the gradient (or $\frac{\partial}{\partial .}$) of the log of the policy π_θ.

This gives

$$\nabla E_{\pi_\theta} \big[r(\tau) \big] = E_{\pi_\theta} \big[r(\tau) \nabla \log \pi_\theta (\tau) \big] \quad (4.8)$$

The following results are needed for calculating this.

- $\pi_\theta(\tau) = P(s_0) \prod_{t=1}^{T} \pi_\theta (a_t \mid s_t) P(s_{t+1}, r_{t+1} \mid s_t, a_t)$ $\qquad (4.9)$

- $\nabla \log \pi_\theta (\tau) = \sum_{t=1}^{T} \nabla \log \pi_\theta (a_t \mid s_t)$ $\qquad (4.10)$

Giving us the following final expression:

$$\nabla E_{\pi_\theta} \big[r(\tau) \big] = E_{\pi_\theta} \left[r(\tau) \left(\sum_{t=1}^{T} \nabla \log \pi_\theta (a_t \mid s_t) \right) \right]$$

$$= \sum_{t=1}^{T} \int r(\tau) \pi_\theta (a_t \mid s_t) \nabla \log \pi_\theta (a_t \mid s_t) d\tau \quad (4.11)$$

This result is independent of the ergodic distribution of states and the environment dynamics. It leads to '*model-free algorithms*' bypassing the need to 'model' the environment. The integral can be calculated by sampling many trajectories and averaging them out. This method is known as Markov Chain Monte-Carlo (MCMC), widely used in probabilistic graphical models and Bayesian networks to approximate parametric probability distributions.

4.2.2 Pseudocode

DQN combines Q-learning with a deep convolutional NN (CNN) specialized for data arrays. For continuous case the Q-function is approximated by deep neural networks (DNN) known as deep Q networks (DQN). After receiving a state as an input, it outputs the Q-values of all possible actions for that state. Its input and output layers have sizes of states and actions, respectively. The agent in each state **enters it as an input to the** DQN and chooses the output action with the highest Q-value.

Initialize replay memory D to capacity N.
Initialize action-value function Q with random weights.

for episode = 1; M **do**
    Initialize sequence $s_1 = \{x_1\}$ and preprocessed sequenced
    $\phi_1 = \phi_1(s_1)$
    for t = 1; T **do**
        With probability ϵ select a random action a_t
        otherwise select $a_t = max_a Q^*(\phi(s_t), a; \theta)$
        Execute action a_t in emulator and observe reward r_t and
        image x_{t+1}
        Set $s_{t+1} = s_t, a_t, x_{t+1}$ and preprocess $\phi_{t+1} = \phi(s_{t+1})$
        Store transition $(\phi_t, a_t, r_t, \phi_{t+1})$ in D
        Sample random minibatch of transitions $(\phi_j, a_j, r_j, \phi_{j+1})$
        from D
        Set $y_j = r_j$ (for terminal ϕ_{t+1})

$$= r_j + \gamma \, max_{a'} Q\left(\phi_{j+1}, a'; \theta\right) \text{ (for non-terminal } \phi_{t+1})$$

        Perform a gradient descent step on $\left(y_j - Q\left(\phi_j, a_j; \theta\right)\right)^2$

    end for
  end for

Source: 'Playing Atari with Deep Reinforcement Learning,' Volodymyr Mnih Koray Kavukcuoglu, David Silver, Alex Graves, Ioannis Antonoglou, Daan Wierstra, and Martin Riedmiller, DeepMind Technologies.

4.2.3 Applications

DQN is one of the most widely used algorithms and has many applications. A brief and incomplete list below tells us about its range and capabilities.

- *Robotics and automation*: DQNs have been used in training robots for tasks ranging from simple object manipulation to assembly tasks in manufacturing processes. We have:
  - The robot states: (i) position and orientation of the robotic arm, (ii) the gripper's state (open or closed), and (iii) the relative position of the objects of interest.
  - The actions: (i) the incremental movements in the joints of the robot arm, or (ii) gripper control commands.
  - The reward function: positive (the arm correctly picks up, moves, or assembles an object), negative (for dropping items or incorrect placement).

  DQN implementation requires a model of the environment, e.g., a real-world interface to a physical robot arm, or a simulated environment and training with a carefully designed reward function and sufficient exploration of the state-action space.

- *Autonomous vehicles and drones*: DQNs are increasingly being used to train cars and drones for safe and efficient navigation in their environments.
  - For self-driving cars, (i) the states are sensor data from LIDAR and RADAR readings, camera images, GPS data, and internal car status data; (ii) the actions are driving maneuvers such as accelerating, braking, or steering; (iii) the reward function is positive for safe and

efficient driving, and negative for traffic rule violations or unsafe driving behaviors.

- For drones, (i) the state includes information about the drone's position, velocity, orientation, battery status, and data from onboard sensors (like cameras or depth sensors); (ii) the actions are commands for changing in thrust and torque for each rotor (for quadcopters); and (iii) the reward function is positive for efficient navigation to the target, and negative for crashes or unsafe flight behavior.

- *Home and industrial automation*: In home automation, DQNs can learn user habits and control smart home devices efficiently.

  - For smart homes, (i) states are the time of day, whether residents are at home, which devices are currently on, and the current energy cos; (ii) the actions are commands, e.g., adjust a thermostat, turn lights on or off, start a washing machine, etc.; (iii) the reward function is better energy efficiency and user comfort preferences.

  - For manufacturing automation, (i) states for optimizing production schedules are manufacturing line, current work orders, historical data etc., and in logistics, states can be the configurations of autonomous forklifts or conveyor systems, etc.; (ii) actions for automation maximize efficiency and minimize downtime, etc., and for logistics they optimize the efficient movement of goods within a warehouse; (iii) the reward function these and similar cases improve operational efficiency, reduce costs, and maintain safety standards. The actual implementation of DQNs would have to manage high-dimensional state and action spaces, delayed rewards, and the need for safe exploration.

- *Personalized medical treatment recommendations*: (i) the states are patient-specific factors such as age, gender, preexisting conditions, genetic information, progression of the disease, etc., (ii) the actions are various treatment options such as medications, dosages, surgery, or other therapies, etc.; (iii) the reward are better patient outcomes to maximize the effectiveness of treatment and minimize side effects or complications, etc.

- *Financial portfolio management and trading:* For trading strategies and managing portfolios, (i) the states are current portfolio holdings, recent market trends, relevant economic indicators, etc., (ii) the actions are buying, selling, holding different assets, etc., (iii) the reward is the profitability of these actions.

The new applications of DQN are being discovered and utilized as machine learning spreads through different activities.

4.3 STATE-ACTION-REWARD-STATE-ACTION (SARSA)

Algorithm	Model	Action	Policy	Perf. Meas.
SARSA	Model-free	discrete	Discrete, on	Q-function

A SARSA agent follows an *on-policy learning algorithm* in which it interacts with the environment and updates modifiable parameters after each visit of a state. The acronym for the quintuple $(s_t, a_t, r_t, s_{t+1}, a_{t+1})$ is SARSA.

In on-policy learning a single policy function is used for (downward) action selection and (upward) value backup towards the learning target. SARSA is an on-policy algorithm, and it updates values directly on the single policy. The same policy function is used for exploration behavior and for the target policy. The SARSA update is given by

$$Q(s_t, a_t) \leftarrow Q(s_t, a_t) + \alpha[r_{t+1} + \gamma Q(s_{t+1}, a_{t+1}) - Q(s_t, a_t)]$$

$$(4.12)$$

And it looks very much like TD, although it uses state-action values, whereas TD deals with state values.

On-policy learning selects an action, evaluates it in the environment, and moves on to better actions, guided by the behavior policy. It samples the state space with a given behavior policy, and improves that by backing up values of the selected actions. Note that the term $Q(s_{t+1}, a_{t+1})$ can also be written as $Q(s_{t+1}, \pi(s_{t+1}))$, highlighting the difference with off-policy learning. SARSA updates its Q-values using the Q-value of the next state s and the current policy's action. The primary advantage of on-policy learning is that it directly optimizes the target of interest and converges quickly by learning with direct behavior values. The sample inefficiency is usually its biggest drawback.

4.3.1 Mathematical Formulation

The Q-function for a state-action is updated by an error, adjusted by the learning rate α.

$$Q^{new}(s_t, a_t) = Q(s_t, a_t) + \alpha\left[r_t + \gamma Q(s_{t+1}, a_{t+1}) - Q(s_t, a_t)\right]$$

(4.13)

Q-functions represent the possible reward received in the next time step for taking the action a_t in state s_t, plus the discounted future reward received from the next state-action observation. SARSA itself learns the Q-function associated with taking the policy it follows.

4.3.2 Pseudocode

The algorithm consists of the following steps:

> At time t:
>> Start in the current state s_t,
>> Choose the action a_t,
>> Get the reward r_t for choosing this action,
> At next time step t+1,
>> enter the state s_{t+1} after taking that action, and finally
>> choose the next action a_{t+1} in its new state.

4.3.3 Applications

SARSA has been used to train robots for autonomous driving, gaming agents to play chess and other games, autonomous vehicles to drive in complex environments.

4.4 SARSA-λ

Algorithm	Model	Action	Policy	Perf. Meas.
SARSA-λ	Model-free	Discrete	Discrete, on	Q-function

The signifier λ in *SARSA-λ* refers to the 'eligibility traces' $e_t(s,a)$. They are mathematical objects designed to improve the convergence of temporal difference (TD) methods and are used in implementing online Monte Carlo and in problems without episodes. They offer improved computational efficiency by

  i. Using a short-term memory vector,

 ii. **Storing a single vector memory** instead of a list of feature vectors, and

iii. Learning continuously rather than waiting for results at the end of an episode.

4.4.1 Mathematical Formulation

Consider the following multi-step returns at some time-step t:

$$q_t^{(1)} = r_{t+1} + \gamma Q_\pi\left(s_{t+1}, a_{t+1}\right)(\text{SARSA}) \qquad (4.14)$$

$$q_t^{(2)} = r_{t+2} + \gamma^2 Q_\pi\left(s_{t+2}, a_{t+2}\right) \qquad (4.15)$$

$$\cdots$$

$$q_t^{(k)} = r_{t+1} + \gamma r_{t+2} + \ldots + \gamma^{k-1} r_{t+k} \ldots + \gamma^k Q_\pi\left(s_{t+k}, a_{t+k}\right) \qquad (4.16)$$

$$\cdots$$

$$q_t^{(\infty)} = r_{t+1} + \gamma r_{t+2} + \ldots + \gamma^{T-1} r_T \ (\text{MC}) \qquad (4.17)$$

As we can see, the process covers returns of all the steps from SARSA to Monte Carlo (MC). In SARSA(λ) one combines them to reach a middle ground between those two methods to exercise control over the bias/variance trade-off. We define a return q^λ giving more weight to closer trajectories and average over multiple n-step returns.

$$q_t^\lambda = (1 - \lambda) \sum_{n=1}^{\infty} \lambda^{n-1} q_t^n \qquad (4.18)$$

Here $\lambda = 0$ is SARSA and $\lambda = 1$ is MC. It allows us to control how far the algorithm should go. For intermediate values of λ, each past experience is given a weight, used for updates called an 'eligibility trace,' one for each function approximator parameter. This strategy generates an exponentially decaying impact of rewards over time.

The expression for updated Q-function is given as

$$Q\left(s_{t+1},\, a_{t+1}\right) = Q\left(s_t,\, a_t\right) + \alpha \delta_t e_t\left(s, a\right) \qquad (4.19)$$

Here

i. $\delta_t = r_{t+1} + \gamma Q\left(s_{t+1}, a_{t+1}\right) - Q\left(s_t, a_t\right)$

ii. $e_t\left(s, a\right) = \gamma \lambda e_{t-1}\left(s, a\right) + 1 \quad$ for $\left(s, a\right) = \left(s_t, a_t\right)$

$\qquad = \gamma \lambda e_{t-1}\left(s, a\right) \qquad$ otherwise

Eligibility trace triggers an update of all recently visited state-action values.

4.4.2 Pseudocode

The algorithm is given below.

Repeat (for each episode): $e_t(s, a)$, for $\forall(s, a)$
Choose initial (s_0, a_0) and $Q(s_0, a_0)$
Repeat (for each episode): Choose action a_t
Observe r_{t+1} and s_{t+1} using policy derived from Q-function

$$\delta_t \leftarrow r_{t+1} + \gamma Q\big(s_{t+1}, a_{t+1}\big) - Q\big(s_t, a_t\big)$$

$$e_t(s, a) \leftarrow \gamma \lambda e_{t-1}(s, a) + 1 \text{ for } \forall(s, a)$$

$$Q\big(s_{t+1}, a_{t+1}\big) \leftarrow Q\big(s_t, a_t\big) + \alpha \delta_t e_t(s, a)$$

Until s_t is terminal

4.4.3 Applications

SARSA-λ has been used to train robots for similar tasks as regular SARSA algorithms.

4.5 ADVANTAGE ACTOR CRITIC (A2C)

Algorithm	Model	Action	Policy	Perf. Meas.
A2C	Model-free	Continuous	Continuous	Value functions and policy optimizations

The RL methods belong to two broad classes of methods.

i. Based on value functions:
It assigns each state-action pair to a value. The critic is a value-based neural network, and it measures how good the action is.

ii. Based on optimizing the policies directly without using value functions:

The actor is a policy-based neural network, and it controls the RL agent's action. Both run in parallel and the real-time feedback from critic improves the actor.

Actor critic methods like A2C (also A3C and SAC) combine both approaches.

In general, the Actor module of the system decides the next action to take. It is not aware if the action is the best possible in the given environment. Now the Critic module enters the scene and evaluates the proposed action's optimality. It also suggests how the actor should adjust the parameters to maximize the reward. This approach is especially important when the environment is dynamic.

In A2C, the value function is the advantage function.

$$A(s_t, a_t) = Q(s_t, a_t) - V(s_t) \qquad (4.20)$$

Where

- $Q(s_t, a_t)$ = the Q-value for the action or maximum future reward in that state
- $V(s_t)$ = the average value of that state.

A positive advantage pushes the gradient in that direction and vice versa.

4.5.1 Mathematical Formulation

Finding a good baseline using state value and computing it is not straightforward either. Let us approximate it using one more parameter ω and denote it by the bootstrapped return $V^\omega(s)$. This idea leads to the Actor-Critic methods in which there are two entities called 'Actor' and 'Critic' defined by functions $\pi_\theta(a_t \mid s_t)$ and $V^\omega(s)$, respectively. One must compute both gradients now.

Define $G_t \cong R_{t+1} + \gamma V^\omega\left(s_{t+1}\right)$ (4.21)

Here

- G_t = a single step bootstrapped return,
- R_{t+1} = is the immediate reward,
- $V^\omega\left(s_{t+1}\right)$ = bootstrapped value-estimate of the next state in the trajectory.

The actor's gradient is calculated as

$$\nabla E_{\pi_\theta}\left[r(\tau)\right] = E_{\pi_\theta}\left[\left(\sum_{t=1}^{T}\left[G_t - V^\omega\left(s_t\right)\right]\nabla \log \pi_\theta\left(a_t \mid s_t\right)\right)\right]$$ (4.22)

The critic's objective $J(\omega)$ is generally taken to be the mean squared error (MSE) or a less harsh Huber loss.

Critic's objective

as MSE: $J(\omega) = \frac{1}{2}\left[G_t - V^\omega\left(s_t\right)\right]^2$ (4.23)

as Huber loss:

$$J(\omega) = \frac{1}{2}\left[G_t - V^\omega\left(s_t\right)\right]^2, for \mid G_t - V^\omega\left(s_t\right)\mid \leq \delta,$$

$$= \delta\left|G_t - V^\omega\left(s_t\right)\right| - \frac{1}{2}\delta^2 \text{ otherwise}$$ (4.24)

The critic's parameters ω is updated by using Stochastic gradient descent (SGD) giving the Critic's gradient as

$$\nabla J(\omega) = G_t - V^\omega\left(s_t\right) \text{ for MSE}$$ (4.25)

4.5.2 Pseudocode

Initialize parameters (s, θ, w) and learning rates (α_θ, α_w)
Sample $a \sim \pi_\theta(a \mid s)$

for $t = 1, \ldots, T$: **do**
    Sample reward $r_t \sim R(s, a)$ and next state $s' \sim P(s' \mid s, a)$
    Sample the next action $a' \sim \pi_\theta(a' \mid s')$
    Update $\theta \leftarrow \theta + \alpha_\theta Q_w(s, a) \nabla_\theta \log \pi_\theta(a \mid s)$
    Compute TD error $\delta_t = r_t + \gamma Q_w(s', a') - Q_w(s, a)$
    Update Q-function parameter $w \leftarrow w + \alpha_w \delta_t \nabla_w Q_w(s, a)$
    Move to $a \leftarrow a'$ and $s \leftarrow s'$
  At next time step $t+1$,
    enter the state s_{t+1} after taking that action, and finally
end for

Based on Lilian Weng's post 'Policy Gradient algorithms.'
At each step, both Critic and the Actor networks are updated.

4.5.3 Applications

A2C networks have been used to train robots for similar tasks as other similar algorithms.

4.6 ASYNCHRONOUS ADVANTAGE ACTOR CRITIC (A3C)

Algorithm	Model	Action	Policy	Perf. Meas.
A3C	Model-free	Continuous	Continuous	Value functions and policy optimizations

The A3C was developed by Google DeepMind and became public in 2016. Unlike DQN which uses a single agent, it uses many agents, each with its own network parameters and a copy of the same environment. Their interaction with the environment is not coordinated globally, so it is 'asynchronous,' hence the name. Each agent is controlled by a global network, so it allows for experimenting with more diversified environment. This mitigates the problem of RL sample correlation.

Just like in A2C, the A3C agent learns the Value Function from the critic and updates its or actor's optimal policy function. It determines the conditional probability for choosing action a in state s and uses Advantage Function to determine how much better the rewards were compared to its expectation. The asynchronous (parallel and distributed) gradient descent is used for optimization of DNN controllers. The training stage uses parallel networks efficiently and independently by adjusting the direction of each training thread. In this way, multiple actor-learners instantiate the environment separately, collect experience, update the gradients, and send it to a central target network. It was found that this parallel operation stabilizes the training.

4.6.1 Mathematical Formulation

It is the same as in A2C but is parallelized for many actors independently and later combined for central update.

4.6.2 Pseudocode

Initialize parameters (s, θ, w) and learning rates (α_θ, α_w)
Sample $a \sim \pi_\theta(a \mid s)$
input:
assume (globally shared) parameter vectors θ and $\phi = 0$,
counter $T = 0$
assume thread-specific parameter vectors θ' and ϕ'
initialize thread step counter $t \leftarrow 1$
repeat
    reset gradients: $d\theta \leftarrow 0$ and $d\phi \leftarrow 0$.
    synchronize thread-specific parameters $\theta' = \theta$ and $\phi' = \phi$

    $t_{start} = t$

    get state s_t
    repeat
        choose action a_t wrt policy $\pi(a_t \mid s_t; \theta')$
        receive reward r_t and new state s_{t+1}

$t \leftarrow t+1$ and $T \leftarrow T+1$

until terminal s_t or $t - t_{start} = t_{max}$

$R = 0$ (for terminal s_t) or $V(s_t, \phi')$ (for non-terminal s_t)

for $i \in (t-1, \ldots, t_{start})$ **do**

$\quad R \leftarrow s_t + \gamma R$

accumulate gradient.

wrt θ': $d\theta \leftarrow d\theta + \nabla_{\theta'} log \pi(a_i \mid s_i; \theta')(R - V(s_i; \phi'))$

wrt ϕ': $d\phi \leftarrow d\phi + \partial(R - V(s_i; \phi'))^2 / \partial\phi'$

end for

update asynchronously θ using $d\theta$ and ϕ using $d\phi$

until $T > T_{max}$

4.6.3 Application

A3C has been found to stabilize the training and surpassed the performance of earlier methods in Atari game environment, motor control problems, and navigating 3D mazes.

4.7 SOFT ACTOR CRITIC (SAC)

Algorithm	Model	Action	Policy	Perf. Meas.
SAC	Model-free	Continuous	Continuous	Value functions

SAC attains SOTA performance in continuous control tasks, e.g., robotic locomotion and manipulation by maximizing the 'entropy' in policy and the expected reward from the environment. This approach encourages the state space exploration, improves the transition data collection, and prevents premature convergence to bad local optima by allowing good policies.

4.7.1 Mathematical Formulation

A two-step *policy iteration technique* alternating between policy evaluation and policy improvement is used. Starting from a given initial policy π, some metric between the current policy and the derived update policy is minimized. Specially in tabular case, an exact solution to MDP can be found by alternating between policy evaluation and policy improvement.

i. In the *policy evaluation* step, the accurate value function for current policy is found by repeatedly evaluating the Bellman operator T_π.

$$[T_\pi V](s) = E_{a\sim\pi(\cdot|s)}\left[r(s,a) + \gamma E_{s'|s,a}\left[V(s')\right]\right] \quad (4.26)$$

For *soft policy iteration*, the policy's entropy as an additional reward term is added to the original Bellman operator.

$$\left[T_\pi Q(s_t,a_t)\right] = r(s_t,a_t) + \gamma E_{a'\sim\pi}$$
$$\left[Q(s_{t+1},a') - \log\pi(a'|s_t)\right] \quad (4.27)$$

Its repeated application to any initial Q function is guaranteed to converge to the optimal 'Soft' Q function.

ii. In the *policy improvement* step, the Bellman optimality operator T is applied repeatedly on given initial value function V so that it converges to the true (optimal) value function V^*.

$$[T*V] = max_\pi\left[T_\pi V\right] \quad (4.28)$$

The optimal policy π^* can be constructed from the optimal value function V^*. For the *soft policy improvement* step, the Kullback–Leibler (KL) distance ('divergence') $J(\omega)$ between the two distributions is minimized.

$$J(\omega) = E\left[KL(\pi(\cdot|s_t)\|\frac{expQ(s,\cdot)}{\sum_a expQ(s,\cdot)}\right] \quad (4.29)$$

This leads to an improved policy.

$$\pi_{new} = argmin_\omega J(\omega) \quad (4.30)$$

This update scheme guarantees monotonic improvement of the policy in the tabular case. In an alternate scheme, NN calculates *Soft Q-function* as the mean and variance with the current state as input, and *Soft Policy* as a Gaussian distribution with the mean and variance from above.

4.7.2 Alternate Method

Both Q-function and policy parameters are updated with the experience data collected from a policy different from the current one. For every actor roll-out, all the transition data is saved in a replay buffer D.

i. *Q-function optimization:* It is done at every update step by using the gradient of the mean squared loss between the predicted action-value and the target action-value q_t.

$$J_Q(\theta) = E_{(s_t,a_t) \sim D} \left[\frac{1}{2} \left(Q_\theta(s_t, a_t) - q_t \right)^2 \right] \quad (4.31)$$

where

$$q_t = E_{a \sim \pi_\omega(\cdot|s_{t+1})} \left[r(s_t, a_t) + Q_\theta(s_{t+1}, a) - \alpha \log \pi_\omega(a'|s_{t+1}) \right] \quad (4.32)$$

Here the α-term represents the 'entropy temperature,' i.e., weight given to the 'randomness' of policy versus the reward from the environment.

ii. *Policy update:* The actions are the hyperbolic tangent Gaussian policy parameters sampled from the mean and covariance output of the policy neural network.

$$a_t = \tanh(u) \quad (4.33)$$

Also, the action is modified as:

$$\log \pi(a \mid s) = \log \mu(u \mid s) - \sum_{i=1}^{D} \log\left(1 - tanh^2\left(u_i\right)\right) \quad (4.34)$$

The $\log \mu(u \mid s)$ represents the cumulative distribution function (CDF) computed with the mean and variance from the policy neural network. The policy parameter can be optimized by minimizing a simplified form of the KL divergence.

$$J_\pi(\omega) = E_{s_t \sim D}\left[E_{a' \sim \pi_\omega(\cdot|s_t)}\left\{\alpha \log \pi_\omega\left(a_t \mid s_t\right) - Q_\theta\left(s_t, a_t\right)\right\}\right] \quad (4.35)$$

The parameter α is updated through the gradient of the objective function including the desired minimum entropy $\bar{H}$ given below:

$$J_\alpha = E\left[-\pi_t\left(a_t \mid s_t; \alpha\right) - \alpha\bar{H}\right] \quad (4.36)$$

4.7.3 Pseudocode
It is like the Actor-Critic case given earlier with appropriate modifications.

4.7.4 Applications
It has been found to be very successful in robotic applications.

4.8 DEEP DETERMINISTIC POLICY GRADIENTS (DDPG)

Algorithm	Model	Action	Policy	Perf. Meas.
DDPG	Model-free	Continuous	Off-policy	Like deep Q-learning

Often one encounters a situation in which the policy is differentiable, but actions are non-stochastic. It becomes then harder to build a policy, and in these cases an action for a given state is learnt directly by a maximization objective.

$$\mu^{k+1} = argmax_a Q^{\mu^k}(s, a) \qquad (4.37)$$

In general, this maximization is computationally hard as one must search the entire space for a given action-value function. An algorithm known as *Deterministic Policy Gradient* (DPG) has handled such situations in which the *argmax* is approximated by a function *approximator*. Its realization using NN is called DDPG.

4.8.1 Mathematical Formulation

The DPG algorithm can be expressed using the following equations.

- Q-learning is minimized with the MSBE loss with SGD.

$$L(\phi, D) = E_{(s,a,r,s',d) \in D} \sum_{(s,a,r,s',d) \in B} \left(Q_\phi(s,a) - y(r,s',d) \right)^2 \quad (4.38)$$

$$y(r,s',d) = r + \gamma(1-d) Q_{\phi_{targ}} \left(s', \mu_{\theta_{targ}}(s') \right) \quad (4.39)$$

- Policy learning is solved by gradient ascent for policy parameters.

$$max_\theta E_{s \in D} Q_\phi \left(s, \mu_\theta(s) \right) \qquad (4.40)$$

4.8.2 Pseudocode

Input: Initialize parameters θ (policy), ϕ (Q-function) and D (empty relay buffer)

Set target and main parameters as equal, i.e., $\theta_{targ} \leftarrow \theta$, $\phi_{targ} \leftarrow \phi$

Repeat:

Observe state s, select action $a = Clip[\mu_\theta(s) + \epsilon, a_{low}, a_{high}]$, with ϵ Gaussian
Execute a∞, observe next state s', reward r, and determine if s' is terminal from signal d
Store (s, a, r, s', d) in replay buffer D, if s' is terminal then reset environment state.
If updating **then**
  For however many updates **do**
    Randomly sample a batch of transitions $B = (s, a, r, s', d)$ from D

    Compute: $y(r, s', d) = r + \gamma(1 - d)Q_{\phi_{targ}}\left(s', \mu_{\theta_{targ}}(s')\right)$

    Update Q-function: $\nabla_\phi \frac{1}{|B|} \sum_{(s,a,r,s',d)\in B} \left(Q_\phi(s,a) - y(r,s',d)\right)^2$

    Update policy: $\nabla_\phi \frac{1}{|B|} \sum_{s\in B} Q_\phi(s, \mu_\theta(s))$

    Update target networks: $\phi_{targ} \leftarrow \rho\phi_{targ} + (1 - \varrho)\phi$,

    $\theta_{targ} \leftarrow \rho\theta_{targ} + (1 - \varrho)\theta$

  End for
 End if
Until convergence

4.8.3 Applications

DDPG has been applied to a wide range of continuous control problems, including robotics, gaming, and autonomous navigation, e.g., robot arm control, autonomous navigation in high-dimensional state spaces, video games with DRL agent, etc.

4.9 TWIN-DELAYED DEEP DETERMINISTIC POLICY GRADIENTS (TD3PG)

Algorithm	Model	Action	Policy	Perf. Meas.
TD3PG	Model-free	Continuous	Off policy	Value function

Just like DDPG, the TD3PG algorithm is also an actor-critic RL agent. It extends the DDPG by reducing the value function overestimates. The significant features of a TD3PG agent are:

- It learns two Q-value functions and uses the minimum of the two for policy updates.
- It updates the policy and targets less frequently than the Q functions.
- It adds noise to the target action during policy updates, which makes the policy less likely to exploit actions with high Q-value estimates.
- It can implement both TD3 and delayed TD3 algorithms. The latter uses only one Q-value function with smoothing of the target policy and delayed policy and target updates.

4.9.1 Mathematical Formulation

The TD3PG algorithm is a slightly modified form of the DDPG one. It can be expressed with the following equations.

- Add a Gaussian noise in the initialized action and update reward with this included. $y \leftarrow r + \gamma min_{i=1,2} Q_{\theta_i}\left(s', \tilde{a}\right)$

- Update critic with loss function.

$$\theta_i \leftarrow argmin_{\theta_i} N^{-1} \Sigma \left(y - Q_{\theta_i}\left(s, a\right)\right)^2 \qquad (4.41)$$

- Update actor with the deterministic policy gradient.

$$\nabla_\phi J(\phi) = N^{-1} \sum_a \nabla_a Q_{\theta_1}(s,a)|_{a=\pi_\phi(s)} \nabla_\phi \pi_\phi(s) \quad (4.42)$$

4.9.2 Pseudocode

Input: Initialize (i) critic Q-functions $\left(Q_{\theta_1}, Q_{\theta_2}\right)$ and actor π_ϕ (policy) with random parameters, (ii) target networks with

$\theta'_1 \leftarrow \theta_1$, $\theta'_2 \leftarrow \theta_2$, $\phi' \leftarrow \phi$, and (iii) target buffer B.
for t=1 **to** T **do**

    select action with Gaussian noise $a \sim \pi_\phi(s) + \epsilon$, observe

    reward r and new state s'
    store (s,a,r,s') in buffer B

    sample a small set of N transitions $(s,a,r,s')\dfrac{-b \pm \sqrt{b^2 - 4ac}}{2a}$
    from B

    $\tilde{a} \leftarrow \pi_{\phi'}(s') + \epsilon'$, $\epsilon \sim clip[\, N(0, \tilde{\sigma}), -c, c]$,

    $y \leftarrow r + \gamma min_{i=1,2} Q_{\theta_i}(s', \tilde{a})$

    update critics $\theta_i \leftarrow argmin_{\theta_i} N^{-1} \sum \left(y - Q_{\theta_i}(s,a)\right)^2$

    if t mod d **then**

        update ϕ by the deterministic policy
        gradient $\nabla_\phi J(\phi) = N^{-1} \sum_a \nabla_a Q_{\theta_1}(s,a)|_{a=\pi_\phi(s)} \nabla_\phi \pi_\phi(s)$

        update target networks $\theta'_i \leftarrow \tau\theta_i + (1-\tau)\theta'_i$,
        $\phi' \leftarrow \tau\phi + (1-\tau)\phi'$
    end if
end for

4.9.3 Applications

TD3PG has been applied to gain further improvements in the solutions to similar problems as handled by DDPG in general.

4.10 TRUST REGION POLICY OPTIMIZATION (TRPO)

Algorithm	Model	Action	Policy	Perf. Meas.
TRPO	Continuous	Continuous or discrete	On-policy	Advantage fn.

It is a DRL algorithm using Stochastic gradient (SG) method to implement trust region update. It guaranteed policy improvement by a local approximation to the loss function due to the new policy.

4.10.1 Mathematical Formulation

Let us begin with given quantities: (i) expected discounted reward $\eta(\pi)$, (ii) visitation frequency $\rho_\pi(s)$, (iii) advantage function $A_\pi(s \mid a)$, and (iv) policy function $\pi(a \mid s)$. Then the TRPO loss function is written as

$$L_\pi\left(\pi_{new}\right) = \eta\left(\pi_{old}\right) + \sum_s \rho_{\pi_{old}}(s) \sum_a \pi_{new}(a \mid s) A_{\pi_{old}}(s \mid a) \quad (4.43)$$

More explicitly, the TRPO approach maximizes an objective function.

a. It is initially $max_\theta L^{CPI}(\theta)$, where $L^{CPI}(\theta) = \widehat{E}_t\left[r_t(\theta)\widehat{A}_t\right]$ = Loss function due to conservative policy iteration with

$\widehat{E}_t[...]$ = the empirical average over a finite batch of samples alternating between sampling and optimization, and

$\widehat{A}_t$ = estimator of advantage function at step t =

$$Q^\pi\left(s_t, a_t\right) - V^\pi\left(a_t\right)$$

b. It is modified by a constraint bound by KL divergence (D_{KL}) over trust region $max_\theta \hat{E}_t\left[r_t(\theta)\hat{A}_t\right]$, such that $D_{KL}\left\{\pi_{\theta_{old}}(.|s_t), \pi_{\theta_{new}}(.|s_t)\right\} \leq \delta$, and $\left(\theta_{old}, \theta_{new}\right)$ = (old, new) vector of policy parameters.

c. For a better result, it is sometimes replaced by an unconstrained optimization: $max_\theta \hat{E}_t\left[r_t(\theta)\hat{A}_t - \beta D_{KL}\left\{\pi_{\theta_{old}}(.|s_t), \pi_{\theta_{new}}(.|s_t)\right\}\right]$ with β as a numerical coefficient and $r_t(\theta) = \dfrac{\pi_{\theta_{new}}(a_t|s_t)}{\pi_{\theta_{old}}(a_t|s_t)}$ = ratio of old and new policy values at time t.

4.10.2 Pseudocode

Input: Initialize (i) policy parameters θ_0, (ii) initial value function parameters ϕ_0, (iii) KL-divergence limit δ, (iv) backtracking coefficient α, and (v) maximum number of backtracking steps K.

for $k = 0,1, 2 ,...$ **do**

run policy $\pi(\theta_k)$, collect trajectories D_k, compute rewards R_t

compute advantage function A_t using current value function V_{ϕ_k}

estimate policy gradient as

$$g_k = \left[\frac{1}{|D_k|}\sum_{\tau \in D_k}\sum_{t=0}^{T}\nabla_\theta log\pi_\theta(a_t|s_t)|_{\theta_k}A_t\right]$$

Use the conjugate gradient algorithm to compute

$$x_k \approx H_k^{-1}g_k$$

(H_k = Hessian of the sample-averaged KL-divergence.)

Backtrack line search to update the policy with

$$\theta_{k+1} = \theta_k + \alpha^j \left(\sqrt{\frac{2\delta}{x_k^T H_k x_k}} \right) x_k \, , \; j \in \{0,1,2,\ldots,K\}$$

(j = the smallest value for improving sample loss while satisfying KL-div. constraint)
Use MSE regression to fit the value function via some gradient descent algorithm:

$$\phi_{k+1} = argmin_\phi \frac{1}{|D_k|T} \sum_{\tau \in D_k} \sum_{t=0}^{T} \left(V_\phi(s_t) - R_t \right)^2$$

end for

4.10.3 Applications

Under proper assumptions TRPO is guaranteed to provide monotonic improvement.

4.11 PROXIMAL POLICY OPTIMIZATION (PPO)

Algorithm	Model	Action	Policy	Perf. Meas.
PPO	Continuous	Discrete or Continuous	On-policy	Advantage function

Like TRPO, which uses second-order methods, the PPO also tries to get the biggest possible improvement in policy but uses first-order methods. It has two variations.

- **PPO-Penalty:** It is a KL-constrained update like the TRPO, but penalizes the KL-divergence in the objective function by automatically adjusting the penalty coefficient.

- **PPO-Clip** doesn't use either KL divergence term or any constraint but clips the objective function to remove incentives for the new policy to get far from the old policy.

Here, we'll focus on PPO-Clip.

4.11.1 Mathematical Formulation

The policy is updated using the following expression.

$$\theta_{k+1} = argmax_\theta E_{(s,a)\sim\pi_{\theta_k}} L\left(s,a,\theta_k,\theta\right) \qquad (4.44)$$

One uses minibatch SGD to maximize the objective L given by

$$L\left(s,a,\theta_k,\theta\right) = \min\left(\frac{\pi_\theta}{\pi_{\theta_k}} A^{\pi_{\theta_k}}\left(s,a\right), g\left(\epsilon, A^{\pi_{\theta_k}}\left(s,a\right)\right)\right) \qquad (4.45)$$

Here

$$g\left(\epsilon, A\right) = \left(1+\epsilon\right)A \; for \; A \geq 0, \left(1-\epsilon\right)A \; for \; A < 0 \qquad (4.46)$$

4.11.2 Pseudocode

Input: Initialize (i) policy parameters θ_0, (ii) initial value function parameters ϕ_0.
for $k = 0,1, 2 ,...$ **do**
run policy $\pi(\theta_k)$, collect trajectories D_k, compute rewards R_t
compute advantage function A_t using current value function V_{ϕ_k}
update policy by maximizing PPO-Clip objective:

$$\theta_{k+1} = argmax_\theta \frac{1}{|D_k|T} \sum_{\tau\in D_k} \sum_{t=0}^{T} \min\left(\frac{\pi_\theta}{\pi_{\theta_k}} A^{\pi_{\theta_k}}\left(s,a\right), g\left(\epsilon, A^{\pi_{\theta_k}}\left(s,a\right)\right)\right).$$

via SGD with Adam (a particular SGD variant)
Use MSE regression to fit the value function via some gradient descent algorithm:

$$\phi_{k+1} = argmin_\phi \frac{1}{|D_k|T} \sum_{\tau\in D_k} \sum_{t=0}^{T} \left(V_\phi\left(s_t\right) - R_t\right)^2$$

end for

4.11.3 Applications

The PPO method has been a very successful RL algorithm and is the preferred method for solving identification and classification problems.

4.12 LONG SHORT-TERM MEMORY (LSTM)

Algorithm	Model	Action	Policy	Perf. Meas.
LSTM	Continuous	Discrete or Continuous	On-policy	Advantage function

The general structure of recurrent neural network (RNN) includes input, output, and hidden layers. The last one contains neurons with memory, so it allows information to persist. In general, their information content does not persist for a long time due to vanishing or blowing up of the gradients of the parameters. The LSTM uses a specialized and more capable neuron consisting of three gates for handling time series problems, e.g., planning, and other time-dependent tasks. The three gates of LSTM are:

i. Forget gate: It chooses whether to keep or forget the previous timestamp's information.

ii. Input gate: It adds or updates information.

iii. Output gate: It passes the updated information to the next timestamp.

In addition, the LSTM neuron has two states.

i. Hidden state: Short-term memory with information $H(t)$ at current timestamp and $H(t-1)$ at previous timestamp.

ii. Cell state: Long-term memory with information $C(t)$ at current timestamp and $C(t-1)$ at previous timestamp.

The updating for different states is done using sigmoid, tanh, or other similar functions.

4.12.1 Mathematical Formulation

Let

x_t = input vector at time t,

h_t and h_{t-1} = hidden state or output vector of LSTM unit,

W and U (with appropriate suffixes) = weight matrices for different gates,

b (with appropriate suffixes) = bias vectors for different gates,

$\circledast$ = Operator for the elementwise or Hadamard product,

d and h = Superscripts denoting number of input features and hidden units,

σ_g = sigmoid function,

Then operations at different gates are:

Forget gate $\quad f_t = \sigma_g\left(W_f x_t + U_f h_{t-1} + b_f\right), f_t \in (0,1)^h$

Input gate $\quad i_t = \sigma_g\left(W_i x_t + U_i h_{t-1} + b_i\right), i_t \in (0,1)^h$

Output gate $\quad o_t = \sigma_g\left(W_o x_t + U_o h_{t-1} + b_o\right), o_t \in (0,1)^h$

The hidden state operations are:

Memory cell input activation vector $\quad \tilde{c}_t = \sigma_c\left(W_c x_t + U_c h_{t-1} + b_c\right),$
$$\tilde{c}_t \in (-1,1)^h$$

Cell state vector $\quad c_t = f_t \circledast c_{t-1} + i_t \circledast \tilde{c}_t$

Hidden state or output vector $\quad h_t = o_t \circledast \sigma_h(c_t), h_t \in (-1,1)^h$

4.12.2 Pseudocode

Input: Initialize (i) sequence length = L, (ii) hidden state vector h_t and h_{t-1}
for $i = 0, 1, 2, \ldots L$ **do**
    if $i = 0$
        h_{t-1} = random (), c_{t-1} = random ()
    else

$$h_{t-1} = h_t, \ c_{t-1} = c_t$$

$$f_t = \sigma_g \left(W_f x_t + U_f h_{t-1} + b_f \right)$$

$$i_t = \sigma_g \left(W_i x_t + U_i h_{t-1} + b_i \right)$$

$$o_t = \sigma_g \left(W_o x_t + U_o h_{t-1} + b_o \right)$$

$$\tilde{c}_t = \sigma_c \left(W_c x_t + U_c h_{t-1} + b_c \right)$$

$$c_t = f_t \circledast c_{t-1} + i_t \circledast \tilde{c}_t$$

$$h_t = o_t \circledast \sigma_h(c_t)$$

end for

4.12.3 Applications

The RNNs using LSTM units are trained using gradient descent. They have led to many remarkable successes in playing games and controlling robots.

4.13 GENERATIVE ADVERSARIAL NETWORK (GAN)

Algorithm	Model	Action	Policy	Perf. Meas.
GAN	xx	Continuous	xx	xx

In GAN approach, two networks contest one another for improved outcome in DRL. The given unsupervised learning problem is formulated as a game between two competing networks known as *Generative* and *Discriminative* networks. In this contest gain of one network becomes loss of another one. The overall approach is as follows:

i. *Generative* network or *generator* G generates random synthetic samples from a latent data distribution, e.g., multivariate normal distribution. For image generation, a deconvolutional NN or a deterministic FFNN is used. Its objective is to increase the error rate of the *discriminative* network.

ii. *Discriminative* network *discriminator* D is trained using a known dataset until a desired accuracy is attained. It takes the samples provided by G and tries to distinguish them from the true data distribution by classifying the sample as real or false. For image generation, a convolutional NN is used to map a sample to a binary classification probability.

The GAN game is then formulated as a zero-sum game for the value of the cross-entropy loss between the discriminator's prediction and the identity of the image as real or generated. Independent backpropagation method is used in both networks so that G produces better samples, while D becomes better at recognizing synthetic samples.

4.13.1 Pseudocode

Here D and G denote *discriminator* and *generator,* respectively.

Input: number of steps k for discriminator
for number of training iterations **do**
  for k steps **do**
    generate samples $\{z^{(1)},...,z^{(m)}\}$ from a noise distribution $p_g(z)$
    choose examples $\{x^{(1)},...,x^{(m)}\}$ from data distribution $p_{data}(x)$
    update the discriminator by ascending stochastic gradient:

$$\nabla_{\theta_d} \frac{1}{m} \sum_{i=1}^{m} \left[logD\left(x^{(i)}\right) + log\left(1 - D\left(G(z^{(i)})\right)\right) \right]$$

  end for
  generate samples $\{z^{(1)},...,z^{(m)}\}$ from a noise distribution $p_g(z)$
  update the generator by descending stochastic gradient:

$$\nabla_{\theta_d} \frac{1}{m} \sum_{i=1}^{m} log\left(1 - D\left(G(z^{(i)})\right)\right)$$

  end for

GANs versus *Actor-Critic* (AC) *method*
The AC and GAN methods look similar, but they differ significantly from one another as given in Table 4.1.

TABLE 4.1   GANs versus AC

Properties	GAN	Actor-Critic
Aims	GANs aim to learn the underlying distribution of the data and afterward generate new samples that were not in the original data set. They are typically formulated as a max-min optimization or saddle-point problem.	AC solves a stochastic optimal control problem from data, without prior knowledge of the environment and learns the model of the environment either implicitly or explicitly. The actor (like G) tracks the policy $P(s,a\,|\,\theta)$ (θ = the distribution specific vector of parameters). The critic (like D) tracks the value function representing the 'goodness' of actor's policy.
Convexity	GANs are inherently nonconvex.	ACs are originally convex but their approximate solution is usually nonconvex, e.g., with DL.
Components	In GANs, G approximates the data distribution, and D evaluates the distribution of the generator	In AC, the actor approximates the policy, i.e., the distribution $P(a\,|\,s)$, and the critic evaluates this policy.
Learning	GANs work in an unsupervised learning setting and mimic the distribution of the given data assumed to be independent and identically distributed (i.i.d.).	ACs work in the RL or a sequential decision-making setting — the action chosen at the current step affects the data seen in the future. AC methods explore the environment and learn to act nearly optimally.
Supervision	In GANs, G gets supervision from D and it signals G about how good or bad the generated data are. If D is removed, then G cannot be trained at all.	In ACs, the critic *improves* the supervision to the actor. The actor can be trained without the critic, in which case, one is simply learning the policy by estimating its future reward. The critic helps make this estimation better.

4.13.2 Applications

GANS have been applied to many problems successfully, e.g., image inpainting, super resolution, Steganography or hiding data in images, synthetic data generation for training models, image and video recognition, etc.

4.14 NORMALIZED ADVANTAGE FUNCTION (NAF)

Algorithm	Model	Action	Policy	Perf. Meas.
NAF		Continuous		

Methods for Q-learning can be used for both discrete and continuous cases.

- The optimal Q-function for discrete action sets is given as

$$Q^*\left(s_t, a_t\right) = E_{s'}\left[r_t + \gamma max_{a'} Q^*\left(s', a'\right) \mid s_t, a_t\right] \quad (4.47)$$

The agent goes through a well-defined discrete action space usually given as a table.

- In continuous cases the action selection step requires taking **arg max** over all possible actions.

$$a_t = max_a Q^*\left(s_t, a; \theta\right) \quad (4.48)$$

The Q-learning methods have difficulty in these situations.

Methods like DDPG have been developed to solve this problem with two NN output streams. NAF is another similar method in which the NNs estimate the value and advantage functions separately. The advantage function is expressed as a quadratic function of the state parameters.

$$A(x,u|\theta^A) = -\frac{1}{2}\left[u - \mu(x|\theta^\mu)\right]^T P(x \mid \theta^P)\left[u - \mu(x)|\theta^\mu)\right] \quad (4.49)$$

There are three output streams now:

i. the value function $V\left(x|\theta^V\right)$,

ii. a state-dependent, positive-definite square matrix formed with a lower-triangular matrix L: $P\left(x|\theta^P\right) = L(x \mid \theta^P)L(x \mid \theta^P)^T$, and

iii. the action $\mu\left(x|\theta^\mu\right)$ which always maximizes the Q-function, since it is quadratic in u.

Afterward, these three streams are combined to give the Q-function.

$$Q\left(x,u|\theta^Q\right) = A\left(x,u|\theta^A\right) + V\left(x|\theta^V\right) \quad (4.50)$$

Here $\theta^Q, \theta^A, \theta^V$ are the parameters of the Q-function, value function and the advantage functions, respectively.

4.13.1 Pseudocode

Randomly initialize normalized Q network $Q(x,u \mid \theta^Q)$
Initialize target network Q' with weight $\theta^{Q'} \rightarrow \theta^Q$.
Initialize replay buffer $R \leftarrow 0$.

for episode = 1, M **do**
    Initialize a random process N for action exploration
    Receive initial observation state $x_1 \sim p\left(x_1\right)$

  for t = 1,...,T **do**
    for iteration = 1,...,I **do**
      Select action $u_t = \mu\left(x_t|\theta^\mu\right) + N_t$
      Execute u_t and observe r_t and x_{t+1}
      Store transition $\left(x_t,u_t,r_t,x_{t+1}\right)$ in R

Set $y_i = r_i + \gamma \mathcal{N}'\left(x_{i+1} \mid \theta^{Q'}\right)$

Update θ^Q by minimizing the loss

$$L = \frac{1}{N}\sum_i \left(y_i - Q(x_i, u_i \mid \theta^Q)\right)^2$$

Update the target network: $\theta^{Q'} \leftarrow \tau\theta^Q + (1-\tau)\theta^{Q'}$
end for
end for
end for

4.15 SELF-ORGANIZING MAPS (SOM)

Algorithm	Model	Action	Policy	Perf. Meas.
SOM		Continuous		

A SOM, based on Kohonen map, is applied to unsupervised learning without using backpropagation. It creates a low-dimensional representation (usually two-dimensional) of a higher-dimensional data while preserving its topological structure. It moves its 'neurons' closer to the data points and finds probable clusters by using a neighborhood function for retaining the data topology.

SOMs have only two layers, one for the input and one for the output or the feature map. There is no activation function, so weights pass to output layer unchanged. Both weight and the input vectors have the same dimension. The weights are updated using the processes of competition, cooperation, and adaptation.

i. *Competition*: This step computes the Euclidean distance between each output layer neuron and the input data. The neuron with the lowest distance ('winner') is chosen as the winner.

ii. *Cooperation*: This step chooses the 'neighbors' using a kernel function dependent on time (increment for the new input) and distance (between the winner and target neuron).

iii. *Adaptation*: This step updates the neurons using the following relation

$$w_k = w_k + \eta(t)h_{ik}(t)\left(x^{(n)} - w_k\right) \qquad (4.51)$$

Here

- $\eta(t) = \eta_0 e^{-t/T_1}$ is the learning rate for determining how much the weights must be adjusted.

- $h_{ik}(t) = \exp\left(-\dfrac{d_{ik}^2}{2\sigma^2(t)}\right)$ is the neighborhood kernel function depending on d_{ik} (the distance between the winner and the other neuron) and $\sigma(t)$ (the time-dependent neighborhood size).

- $\sigma(t) = \sigma_0 e^{-t/T_2}$ is the neighborhood size decay rule.

4.15.1 Pseudocode

Randomly initialize weights to some small values.
Repeat until convergence
    Select the next input pattern x^{in} from the database.
    Find the unit w_i that best matches x^{in}

$$i\left(x^{in}\right) = argmin_j \left\| x^{in} - w_j \right\|.$$

Update the weights of winner w_i and its neighbors w_k

$$w_k = w_k + \eta(t).h_{ik}(t).\left(x^{in} - w_k\right)$$

Decrease the learning rate $\eta(t)$ and
neighborhood size $\sigma(t)$

4.16 *REINFORCE* GRADIENT WITH AND WITHOUT BASELINE

Algorithm	Model	Action	Policy	Perf. Meas.
REINFORCE: gradient		Continuous		

*REINFORCE is the acronym for **RE**ward Increment = Non-negative Factor × **O**ffset Reinforcement × Characteristic Eligibility.*

REINFORCE without baseline:
The gradient of policy $\pi_\theta(a_t \mid s_t)$ does not depend on reward $r(\tau)$, but it makes the variance of the MCMC sampling quite large. Define:

G_t = the discounted return,

As the past rewards do not contribute anything, so the policy gradient can be replaced by G_t.

$$\nabla E_{\pi_\theta}\left[r(\tau)\right] = E_{\pi_\theta}\left[\left(\sum_{t=1}^{T} G_t \nabla \log \pi_\theta(a_t \mid s_t)\right)\right] \quad (4.52)$$

This is the basis of the MCMC policy gradient algorithm *REINFORCE.*

It is an MCMC policy gradient algorithm for the episodic case and therefore it requires a complete episode to get the sample proportional to the gradient. It then updates the policy parameter with the step size.

REINFORCE with baseline:
The above algorithm prescription does not totally alleviate the problem related to sampling. It uses the Monte Carlo method which has high variance and consequently slow learning. So, a baseline parameter b is introduced for the gradient to reduce its variance. Then the above expression is modified as:

$$\nabla E_{\pi_\theta}\left[r(\tau)\right] = E_{\pi_\theta}\left[\left(\sum_{t=1}^{T}(G_t - b)\nabla\log\pi_\theta\left(a_t \mid s_t\right)\right)\right] \quad (4.53)$$

It can be proved that

$$E_{\pi_\theta}\left[\left(\sum_{t=1}^{T}b\nabla\log\pi_\theta\left(a_t \mid s_t\right)\right)\right] = 0 \quad (4.54)$$

The baseline parameter b reduces the variance as well as keeps the gradient still unbiased. A good baseline is the current state-value defined as the expected return given a state following the policy π_θ or $V(s) = E_{\pi_\theta}\left[G_t \mid s_t = s\right]$.

CHAPTER 5

Multi-Agent RL (MARL) Algorithms

A S A SUBFIELD OF RL, **multi-agent reinforcement learning (MARL)** studies the behavior of many learning agents coexisting in a shared environment. Each agent seeks its own reward and acts to advance its own interests. There are two cases to distinguish.

- In a cooperative case, MARL agents work together to maximize a given goal.
- In a competitive case, the agent interests are opposed to those of others.

MARL uses the theory of repeated games combined with the pursuit of finding ideal algorithms that maximize rewards. While single-agent RL tries to find the algorithm that gets the biggest rewards for one agent, MARL evaluates and quantifies

DOI: 10.1201/9781032659800-5

social metrics, such as cooperation, reciprocity, equity, social influence, language, and discrimination.

5.1 COOPERATION VERSUS COMPETITION

When many agents share the same environment, their interests might be aligned or misaligned. MARL allows exploring all the different alignments and how they affect the agents' behavior:

- *Pure competition settings*: The agents' rewards are exactly opposite to each other, and therefore they are playing a zero-sum game *against* each other, e.g., games like Go and chess, and projects like AlphaGo and Deep Blue. Neither agent takes actions that benefit its opponent.

- *Pure cooperation settings*: The agents get the exact same rewards, and therefore they are playing *with* each other. MARL approach is used to explore how agents with identical interests can communicate and work together. Pure cooperation settings are explored in recreational cooperative games like Overcooked, and in real-world robotics scenarios. In pure cooperation settings, agents converge to specific 'conventions' when coordinating with each other.

- *Mixed-sum settings*: These cover situations which combine elements of both cooperation and competition, e.g., self-driving cars, such that each car minimizes the time it takes to reach its destination, but all cars have the shared interest of avoiding a traffic collision.

  Classic matrix games such as Prisoner's dilemma and recreational games such as Diplomacy and StarCraft II are good examples. These settings sometime create communication and social dilemmas.

5.2 GENERAL CONSIDERATIONS FOR MARL

5.2.1 Training

The approaches to training must consider the following possibilities:

i. Train all agents independently so that each agent considers all others as part of the environment and learns its own policy in a fully decentralized approach or

ii. Implement *Centralized Learning with Decentralized Execution* (CLDE) in which one takes in the state of the environment and returns an action for each agent in the form of a single joint action vector, thus learning a single policy for all agents.

5.2.2 Single-Agent Setting as Reference

There are many new considerations for implementing DRL algorithms when the number of agents increases beyond 1. We first recall the single-agent situation for further reference. Let an agent at a given time step t

i. be in a state s_t (from state space S) and

ii. choose an action a_t (from action space A) to

iii. transition to state s_{t+1} by

iv. receiving reward r_t.

Then, this agent's value function for policy π is given by the following expression:

$$v_\pi(s_t) = E_\pi\left[\sum_{k=0}^{\infty} \gamma^k r_{k+t+1}\right] \tag{5.1}$$

Here $\gamma \in [0, 1]$ is the discount factor and E_π is the expectation value operator.

The value function for optimal policy $\pi*$ can be obtained by using Bellman's equation.

$$v_\pi^*\left(s_t\right)= max_a \sum_{s^{new}} p(s^{new} \mid s_t,a)\left[r\left(s_t,a\right)+ \gamma v_\pi^*\left(s^{new}\right)\right] \quad (5.2)$$

Similarly, the optimal Q-value is given by appropriate Bellman's equation.

$$Q_\pi^*\left(s_t,a_t\right)= \sum_{s^{new}} p(s^{new} \mid s_t,a_t)\left[r\left(s_t,a_t\right)+ \gamma max_{a^{new}} Q_\pi^*\left(s^{new},a^{new}\right)\right]$$

$$(5.3)$$

Here $p(s^{new} \mid s_t,a_t)$ is the probability of transitioning to the new state s^{new} after taking action a_t in state s_t.

5.2.3 Basic Equations for the Multi-Agent Q-Function Framework

The mathematical framework of the most MARL methods focusses on finding an optimum Q-value and/or policy. For MARL cases, a modified version of the above optimal Q-value equation is the following:

$$Q_x^*\left(s,a_x \mid \boldsymbol{\pi}_{-x}\right)$$
$$= \sum_{a_{-x}} \boldsymbol{\pi}_{-x}\left(a_{-x},s\right)\begin{bmatrix} r\left(s,a_x,\boldsymbol{a}_{-x}\right)+ \gamma\sum_{s^{new}} P(s^{new} \mid s,a_x,\boldsymbol{a}_{-x}) \\ max_{a_x^{new}} Q_x^*\left(s^{new},a_x^{new}\right) \end{bmatrix} \quad (5.4)$$

Here

    i. a_x = the action of agent x

    ii. $\boldsymbol{a}_{-x}$ = the action vector of all agents except agent x.

    iii. $\boldsymbol{\pi}_{-x}$ = the policy vector of all agents except agent x.

    iv. P = the transition probability among the states.

5.2.4 Basic Equations for the Multi-Agent Policy-Function Framework

The above equations can be written using policy as a parameter during learning to optimize a policy-based function. The equation can be solved using policy gradient methods for finding an approximation to the gradient.

The MARL framework is a stochastic game based on the Markov decision process represented formally as:

- Game represented as the tuple S, actions $A_1, A_2, \ldots, A_n$, Rewards $R_1, R_2, \ldots, R_n$, (n = the number of agents), P (transition function)
- $A = A_1 X A_2 X \ldots X A_n$ is the joint action space of all agents,
- $S \times A \times S \rightarrow R$ is the reward function of each agent,
- The state transition function $P : S \times A \times S \rightarrow [0, 1]$
- H = joint policy
- Reward function is bounded.

State transitions are the result of all agents acting together and the rewards depend on the joint policy. The reward R_i^H for the ith agent under the joint policy H is given by:

$$R_i^H = E[R_{t+1} \mid S_t = s, A_{t,i} = a, H] \qquad (5.5)$$

The corresponding Bellman equation for Q-function is:

$$Q_i^H(s,a) = E_i^H[R_{t+1} + \gamma Q_i^H(S_{t+1}, A_{t+1}) \mid S_t = s, A_t = a] \quad (5.6)$$

There is a similar equation for value function.
In general, the stochastic games are of three kinds:

  i. Fully cooperative: All agents have the same reward ($R_1 = R_2 = \ldots = R_n$) and their goal is to maximize it.

ii. Fully competitive: The agents have opposite goals, e.g., for $n = 2$, $R_1 = -R_2$.

iii. Mixed games: The agents' rewards are usually different and correlated.

5.2.5 An Example

There are three primary challenges associated with MADRL. In this example, an approach to their solutions is given which can be used in other similar situations.

- *Problem representation*: We need to represent an arbitrary number of agents without changing the architecture of the deep Q-Network. To solve this problem, a number of simplifying assumptions are made: (i) environment is two-dimensional, (ii) time and space are discrete, and (iii) there are two types of agents (allies and opponents).

  The global system state can be represented as an image-like tensor, with each channel containing agent- and environment-specific information. This representation can now be used to take advantage of convolutional neural networks (CNN) which work well for image classification tasks. The image tensor is of size 4 _W_ H, where W and H are the height and width of our two-dimensional domain and four is the number of channels in the image. Each channel encodes a different set of information from the global state in its pixel values. The channels can be broken down in the following way:

  _ Background Channel: contains information about any obstacles in the environment

  _ Opponent Channel: contains information about all the opponents

  _ Ally Channel: contains information about all the allies

  _ Self Channel: contains information about the agent making the decision

Note that channels in the image-like representation are sparse. In both the opponent and ally channels, each non-zero pixel value encodes the number of opponents or allies in that specific position.

- *Multi-agent training*: When many agents interact in an environment, their actions may directly impact the actions of other agents. So, the agents must be able to reason about one another for intelligent actions. One trains one agent at a time and keeps the policies of all the other agents fixed during this period. After a set number of iterations, the policy learned by the training agent gets distributed to all the other agents of its type. Specifically, an agent distributes its policy to all its allies. In this way one set of agents incrementally improves its policy over time. The learning process itself is not distributed, but the policy execution is distributed, because each agent has its own NN controller. Each agent must be aware of the locations of all the other agents, but it does not need to tell the other agents about its intent.

- *Agent ambiguity*: Consider a scenario where two ally agents occupy the same position in the environment. The image-like state representation for each agent will be identical, so their policies will be the same. To break this symmetry, a stochastic policy for agents is used in which an agent's action is drawn from a distribution. For example, it can be a softmax over the NN's Q-values. This allows allies to take different actions if they occupy the same state and break the ambiguity.

5.3 REWARD MACHINES (RMS) FOR MARL

RM is a kind of reward function generalized to the multi-agent scenario. It encodes a non-Markovian reward in a type of finite-state machine. It takes subsets of propositional variables as input and outputs real numbers as reward values.

RM abstracts the current environment state to sets of high-level events.

- Input: It is the current RM state $u \in U$ and the environment state $s \in S$
- Output: It is a collection of multiple concurrent events which are passed as unordered sequence to the RM. It depends both on the environment and on the current progress through the task specifying local labeling functions.

RMs decompose a complex task into several stages and simplify the stage-specific operations.

Reward functions are part of the MDP formalism of a single RL agent, and they have been generalized to 'Reward Machines' for the case of the multi-agent RL. They use finite state machines (FSM) to allow the team-level task to be decomposed into subtasks for individual agents. Its output value depends on the present state and the current input symbol and can be characterized by the following elements:

  i. A finite set of states,
  ii. An initial state,
  iii. An input alphabet,
  iv. An output alphabet,
  v. A transition function map from (states, input alphabet) to input alphabet, and
  vi. An output function map from (states, input alphabet) to input alphabet. The lengths of input and output are equal.

RMs use a particular form of FSM called 'Mealy' machines for the structured representation of reward functions using concatenations, loops, and conditional rules. Given an RM framework, the agents can separate the team-level tasks into stages and learn the stage-specific behaviors for the overall task. Q-Learning for reward machines (QRM) decomposes the problem to improve sample efficiency and uses q-learning to update each subtask policy in parallel, which guarantees convergence to an optimal policy. QRM can be combined with DRL methods.

5.3.1 Markov Game, Nash Equilibrium, and Pareto Optimality

Markov games (MG) are multi-agent generalization of Markov decision process (MDP), which itself is the basic framework for the single-agent RL. In MG framework, many agents interact simultaneously within a shared environment and with each other. It is given by the following elements:

    i. **A set of interacting agents {1, 2, …, N}, N>1**

    ii. **A set of states observed by all agents** representing all possible agent configurations in the environment,

    iii. **A set of joint actions of** the agents which is a collection of the individual action spaces of all agents,

    iv. **Transition probabilities** for the chance of a state transition,

    v. **Individual rewards**, specific to an agent for arriving at a new state by taking a specific action,

    vi. **A discount factor γ** for diminishing future rewards.

In multi-agent situation, the best response is found by taking multiple reward functions. In general, this may not be the best. That is determined by the *Nash equilibrium*, which is a solution such that no one agent can improve upon the policy when other agents' policies are fixed. This situation of non-uniqueness is called *Pareto optimal*, when no agent action is available that makes one get more reward without making others worse off.

5.3.2 Pareto Optimality

A strategy is called Pareto-optimal or Pareto-efficient if a strategy or policy profile dominates all others if no agent using a chosen strategy profile can be better off without making another agent using the same profile more efficient. A Pareto improvement is defined as any adjustments to a strategy profile that makes the resulting strategy profile more Pareto efficient. So a strategy profile π^* is a Pareto efficient solution if it is not Pareto dominated by any other strategy profiles. It maximizes the overall welfare defined as the sum of all agents' utilities without emphasizing individual rational decisions.

5.3.3 Nash Equilibrium

It is a state in which no individual agent can increase its expected return by unilaterally deviating from their policy. It means that all agent strategies are the best responses to the other agents' strategy. It is not unique and computing it in complex situations may even be impossible. In such situations ϵ-Nash equilibrium is more tractable. It relaxes the requirements by allowing the agent to deviate if it improves its expected returns by more than some value ϵ.

5.3.4 Q-Learning with RMs (QRM)

It is an algorithm that learns a collection of q-functions, one for each RM state $u \in U$, corresponding to the optimal policies for each stage of the task.

A naive approach to applying RMs in the MARL setting would be to treat the entire team as a single agent and use QRM to learn a centralized policy. This approach quickly becomes intractable due to the exponential scaling of the number of states and actions with the number of agents. Furthermore, it assumes agents communicate with a central controller at every time step, which may be undesirable from an implementation standpoint.

A basic RM algorithm for Q-learning is given below (Ref: Neary)

```
Input: R = ⟨ U, u₁ , Σ, δ, σ, F ⟩, L, γ, α
Output: Q = {q_u : S × A → R|u ∈ U}
Q ← InitializeQFunctions ()
for n = 1 to NumEpisodes do
    u₁ ← u₁ , s₁ ← environmentInitialState ()
    for t = 0 to NumStemps do
        a ← getAction (q_{u₁} , s₁)
        s₂ ← executeActions ( s₁, a)
        r, u₂ ← rewardsMachineOutput(u₁, L (s₂ , u₁))
        q_u (s₁, a) ← (1 − α) q_{u₁} (s₁, a) + α (r + γ max_{a'∈A} q_{u₂}
        (s₂ , a'))
    for u ∈ U, u ≠ u₁ do
        r, u' ← rewardMachineOutput (u, L (s₂ , u));
        q_u (s₁, a) ← (1 − α) q_u (s₁, a) + α (r + γ max_{a'∈A} q_{a'}
        (s₂ , a'))
    u₁ ← u₂ , s₁ ← s₂
    if u₁ ∈ F then
        break
return Q
```

The algorithm works as follows:

- The agent starts with RM state u_1 and environment state s_1
- It uses its estimate of q_{u_1} (s_1,.) to select action a.
- The environment goes to state s_2.
- The RM transitions to state u_2 caused by the events output by L (s_2, u_1).
- The agent updates the optimal q-function q_{u_1}(s_1, a) using reward output by σ.
- The agent queries the rewards and RM transitions that would have occurred had the RM been in any other state u and uses this information to update the estimate of each q_u.

The tabular QRM algorithm is guaranteed to converge to an optimal policy.

5.4 MARL ALGORITHMS: NEURO-SYMBOLIC LEARNING

We interact with outside world in a two-tiered manner:

i. Perception through sensory inputs which is mapped into symbols, and

ii. Cognition which maps the symbols into knowledge about the environment.

This is further used for supporting abstraction, reasoning by analogy, and long-term planning.

The NN-based AI algorithms effectively model machine perception, but for modeling human cognition a different approach using symbolic knowledge structure is needed. Neuro-symbolic AI approach supports mapping perception output to knowledge which enables traceability of knowledge systems. It combines NN with knowledge-guided symbolic approaches to create more capable and flexible AI systems capable of combining both algorithm and application-level capabilities.

Further analysis of this approach leads to two major considerations.

Symbolism: It represents objects as symbols and uses rules of logic to work with them. Let A denote the collection of propositions and B the general principles. Then historically three different types of reasoning have been found by logicians for the symbolic approach.

- *Deductive*: One derives A from B only when A is a formal logical consequence of B.
- *Inductive*: One infers B if given A.

- *Abductive*: One infers A as an explanation of B without rigorous logical analysis. This allows preconditions from consequences which is opposite in direction to induction.

It is apparent that all of them involve working with symbols. It requires relatively few input symbols for representing knowledge of the target system and internal functioning of the programs is transparent.

It was discovered soon that the symbolic approach does not work well with noisy and ambiguous real-world data.

Connectionism: It was generally observed that

- Cognitive processes (attention, problem-solving, memory, learning, decision-making, language, perception, imagination, and logic reasoning) arise from neurons and their connections.

- Learning occurs through weight modification, minimizing cumulative error and with discovery of statistical patterns in the input data.

Thus, 'cognition' can be represented as stemming from the interconnected networks of uniform 'neuron'-like units, thus allowing its representation by neural networks (NNs).

Despite many successes, this approach also has some shortcomings like lack of compositional generalization and a verifiable train of logic and no understanding of why a decision was made. Application of this approach to critical areas like medical diagnosis, autonomous driving, and mathematical reasoning has proved very problematic.

Integration of two approaches: *Neuro-Symbolic learning*

Recently, researchers have tried to combine the above two as 'Neuro-symbolic' (**NeSy**) approach to AI. It was also found that neural (N) and symbolic (S) components can be combined in different ways. The following six broad types capture this integration:

i. **S-N-S**: symbols as both input and output.

ii. **S[N]**: neural as subroutine inside overall symbolic approach.

iii. **N|S**: neural and symbolic both at the same co-routine level.

iv. **N:S→N**: symbolic rules integrated with NN's architecture or training.

v. **N_S**: symbolic as soft constraint on loss function in training NN.

vi. **N[S]**: symbolic engine directly embedded inside an NN engine, logical reasoning as tensor calculus.

This is a rapidly evolving area of research and does not have a universally agreed approach yet. Here one such approach will be described to give a general idea of the research in this field.

5.5 MARL FOR A2C AND A3C

This variation of A2C was developed by Google DeepMind. It uses many agents with each having its own copy of the environment. All agents also have their own set of network parameters, which are different from others. They interact with their environments asynchronously and learn with each interaction just like in an A2C algorithms. They learn the conditional probability $P(a \mid s, \theta)$, where θ denotes the agent-specific network parameters. At the same time, they are also controlled by a global network, which collects the learning information and creates a better picture of the environment. This process mimics the human learning process more accurately as we learn from various sources.

5.6 MULTI-OBJECTIVE RL (SINGLE AND MULTI-AGENT)

In most real-world problems, our decisions involve optimization of more than a single objective. For example, in medical situations, we may want to maximize the effectiveness of the treatment, while minimizing a variety of side effects. Most real-world decision problems are inherently multi-objective, and they need a generalization of the single objective RL to multi-objective one. Many times, all the goals needed by an adequate solution are combined into a scalar and additive reward function and numerical rewards or penalties are assigned to events that can occur in the environment.

For single-agent RL, this leads to fine-tuning the reward function iteratively until a satisfactory solution is found. This is an unsatisfactory approach lacking explainability and inability to handle changing requirements. Mathematically, it implies that it is always possible to convert a MOMDP into an MDP. An a priori scalarization function is required for this to work which may or may not be feasible or desirable.

Some scenarios and examples are presented here:

- *Unknown utility function* scenario: There is too much uncertainty about knowing the correct utility function. It is preferable to compute a broader set of policies to respond quickly whenever more information is available.

- *Decision support* scenario: The user's preferences are unknown or difficult to specify. It is almost identical to the unknown utility function scenario. The only difference is that the user selects a policy based on its preference. Capturing preferences and trade-offs for all stakeholders across all objectives is difficult, if not impossible. One solution is to learn a set of optimal policies and let an authority (local council or government) decide what policy to follow after a collective decision has been made by a local council or government.

- *Known utility function* scenario: The user's preferences are known at the time of learning or planning, so scalarization is both possible and feasible. However, sometimes this can lead to an intractable problem. Usually, since the user's preferences are known, it is possible to learn a single optimal policy.

- *Interactive decision support* scenario: The agent learns both the preferences of the user in the given environment. During learning, the agent can find user preferences and remove uncertainty from the user's utility function. At various times during the learning phase a user could be presented with different potential solutions and rank the solutions in order of preference, so the system gets a more accurate representation of the users preferences and learns an optimal solution.

- *Dynamic utility function* scenario: The user's preferences for certain objectives change over time. Therefore, applying a priori scalarization would be undesirable. An optimal approach for the algorithm is to learn a finite number of policies over time and choose an appropriate non-dominated policy for any utility function and improve upon it. Although there is an infinite amount of utility functions, they can be covered by a finite number of policies.

- *Review and adjust* scenario: A user may be uncertain about its objective preferences over time, making utility function too much uncertain. In this scenario, learning a coverage set of policies is optimal, so a user can select the policy accurately reflecting its preferences. The chosen solution can be reviewed before execution. If the user's preferences have changed, selected solution can be adjusted to accurately reflect the updates.

Multi-objective RL tries to overcome these shortcomings. Some useful approaches are:

i. *Stateless/bandit algorithms*:

The well-known *Multi-Armed Bandit* (MAB) algorithm gives an optimal exploration/exploitation strategy for selecting between different actions (arms). The aim is to minimize the regret defined as the loss in reward from not selecting the initially unknown optimal action on every time step). This has been extended to MORL by extending this concept to multi-objective regret in which the agent minimizes the number of Pareto-dominated actions. This general idea has resulted in several MORL algorithms like multi-objective χ-armed bandit (the set of arms is measurable), a modified form of the Hierarchical Optimistic Optimization (HOO) algorithm, multi-objective ranked bandits, etc.

ii. *Single-policy algorithms*:

Extension of existing single-objective model-free value-based methods, such as Q-learning, to multi-objective situation is the most widely adopted approach to MORL. It requires two changes to the learning algorithm.

- The agent stores Q-values as vectors rather than as scalars, and
- The scalarization function has to match the utility function and should be used to identify the greedy action to perform in any given state.

In the case of either weighted or unweighted linear scalarization function, this is equivalent to transforming the MOMDP into a corresponding MDP. Extension to nonlinear case is quite complicated and several approximate methods have been devised.

iii. *Multi-policy algorithms*:

These approaches fall into two classes:

- *Outer loop* methods operate on series of single-objective problems. The simplest outer loop methods iterate through a series of different parameter settings for a utility function and re-run a single-policy MORL method for each setting.
- *Inner loop* methods directly produce multiple policies by modifying the algorithm to directly identify and store multiple-policies in parallel rather than sequentially. Pareto-Q-learning is a good example of this.

In case of continuous state-action spaces and not fully observable states, policy search or actor-critic algorithms have been considered.

CHAPTER 6

Recent Developments in DRL

T HE Deep reinforcement learning – both theory and applications – is developing rapidly. New ideas and techniques are entering discourse very often. In this chapter some of them are presented. The list is not exhaustive but hopefully introduces the readers to some of the intellectual excitement permeating the research in this area.

Table 6.1 identifies some of the popular DRL algorithms underlying recent work.

6.1 PHYSICS-BASED NNS AND DRL

A supervised learning NN is a universal function approximator. However, it is strongly limited if one wants to extrapolate the desired solution for input variable values situated outside the range of the training data. This becomes a bottleneck, when in addition to this, the data is hard to come by due to the nature of

 DOI: 10.1201/9781032659800-6

TABLE 6.1   Some DRL Algorithms

Common Algorithms		Characteristics
Value-based methods	State-Action-Reward-State-Action (SARSA)	Learn Q function through TD learning algorithm and use Q function to generate actions
	Deep Q Network (DQN)	Combining neural network with Q-learning and adopting random strategy, each time learning uses the action that the current strategy believes to be the most valuable, it is easy to overestimate the Q value.
	Double (DQN)	The problem of overestimation is solved by improving the algorithm that separates selection from evaluation.
	Averaged-DQN	By reducing the approximate error variance in the target value, the training process is more stable, and the performance is improved.
	Multiple DQN variant combinations: Rainbow	Combine the six extensions and improvements of DQN algorithm and focus on the same agent, including DDQN, priority-based reuse pool, competitive network, multi-step learning, distributed RL and noise network.
	Action Elimination – DQN (AE-DQN)	To reduce the probability of redundant and uncorrelated actions, a system is proposed to learn the approximate value of Q-function and eliminate actions at the same time, which includes two deep neural networks: DQN and action elimination network.
Policy-based methods	Recurrent Deterministic Policy Gradient (RDPG)	Using RNN, agents can integrate the characteristics of historical information and combine it with deterministic strategy gradient DPG to solve some observable problems in POMDP.

(Continued)

TABLE 6.1 (Continued)

Common Algorithms	Characteristics
Deep Deterministic Policy Gradient (DDPG)	Separate the exploration of action strategies from the learning and updating of action strategies, explore and use random strategies, and learn to use deterministic strategies; Increase batch normalization to prevent gradient explosion.
Trust Reason Policy Gradient(TRPG)	The advantage function is introduced to evaluate the current action value relative to the average value, to solve the problem of inappropriate step selection; The importance sampling processing action distribution is introduced to solve the problem of low data sampling efficiency.
Proximal Policy Optimization (PPO)	Use first-order optimization to minimize the loss function; High stability and good applicability in continuity problems; The implementation is relatively simple.
Model-based methods	Continuous deep Q-learning based on model acceleration	The RL algorithm based on model and without model is effectively combined to improve efficiency.
Exploration with Exemplar Models (EX2)	The novelty is estimated by considering the ease with which the classifier trained by discriminant can distinguish a given state from other states seen previously so as to solve the sparse reward problem.
Model-Ensemble Trust-Region Policy Optimization (ME-TRPO)	With the same performance as the most advanced model-free algorithm, the sample complexity is greatly reduced; Model integration technology is effective in overcoming model deviation. The introduction of tpro makes learning more stable.

TABLE 6.1   (Continued)

Common Algorithms		Characteristics
	Temporal Difference Model(TDM)	Using the relationship between model-based learning and model-free learning to learn specific types of target condition value functions, the sample complexity in continuous control tasks is higher than that in complete model-free learning, and the performance is better than that of pure model algorithm.
Hierarchy-based methods	Hierarchical DRL	Decisions are made at two levels: the top-level module receives the state and selects a new goal, and the low-level module uses the state and the selected goal to make decisions until the goal is achieved or terminated.
	Feudal Network Hierarchy RL	Using different time resolutions, using the manager module and the worker module, it is a consistent, end-to-end differentiable model, using directional rather than absolute goals.
	Hierarchical reinforcement learning based on Stochastic Neural Network	First, learn skills in the pretraining environment and use agent reward signals to reduce the complexity of samples; Training advanced strategies on learning skills can achieve good performance in reward sparse or long horizon tasks.

the problem. In addition, the datasets corresponding to specific boundary conditions, material types, etc., are very hard to generalize to new and unseen situations.

In the past, many NN methods like DNN, RNN, CNN, GAN, and Neural Operators have been used for tackling these problems.

Many times, the underlying system is known to be described by known laws of physics in the form of general partial differential equations (PDEs). Using this information in the learning stage makes it possible to overcome the problem of data scarcity. Physics-inspired NNs lie at the intersection of the pure physics-based system description and pure data-driven explanations. They ensure consistency with known physics of the system and also allow extrapolation beyond the available data.

There are four distinct neural network frameworks based on how the underlying physics is treated.

6.1.1 Physics-Guided Neural Networks (PgNNs)

PgNNs use supervised DL techniques to construct mappings between formatted inputs and outputs generated from experiments and computations in a controlled setting. The mappings are checked extensively to ensure compliance with physics principles and fundamental rules. Such models require a rich and sufficient dataset to be trained and used reliably.

The model maps a set of inputs x to outputs y using an appropriate function F with unknown parameters w such that $y = F(x; w)$. By specifying a particular structure for F, a data-driven approach fine-tunes the parameters w so that the overall error between true and model-predicted values is minimized. The cost of data acquisition for complex physical systems is quite high. This results in sparse data so the vast majority of state-of-the-art PgNNs lack robustness and fail to generalize using interpolation and extrapolation. Some of the other limitations are also important considerations before deciding to use them.

- Their training process is solely based on statistics and generates models based on correlations in statistical variations. The predictions, thus, are naturally physics-agnostic and may violate the underlying physics. The training datasets are usually sparse and do not cover the entire range of underlying experimental attributes.

Therefore, the models also fail in blind testing on conditions outside the scope of training.

- Their predictions might be incorrect, even for inputs within the scope of sparse training datasets due to lack of interpolation capabilities, especially for very wide range of the attributes. Also, they may not fully satisfy the training-specific initial and boundary conditions which vary from one problem to another, making the data generation and training process prohibitively costly. Additionally, inverse problems estimate parameters only indirectly related to these attributes.

- As they are not resolution-invariant by construction, so they cannot be trained on a lower resolution and be directly inferred on a higher resolution because they are only designed to learn the solution of physical phenomena for a single instance (i.e., inputs-outputs). While these models are optimal with respect to the entire dataset, they may produce suboptimal results in individual cases. They may struggle to learn the underlying process for diverse training dataset, i.e., when the interdependencies between different input and output pairs are drastically different.

6.1.2 Physics-Informed NNs (PiNNs)

They are data-driven to learn a model and ensure consistency with the applicable physics. They can generate more robust models with less data and are effective for ill-posed and inverse problems. Using domain decomposition allows scaling them to large problems.

PiNNS remediate the generalizability issue by performing supervised learning tasks while obeying laws of physics given as general nonlinear PDEs or ordinary differential equations (ODEs). They use deep NNs with a series of fully connected layers and a variant of gradient descent optimization. The learning or training process and hyperparameter tuning are conducted manually and depend on problem-dependent sample size.

They incorporate a weakly imposed loss function consisting of the residuals of physics equations and boundary constraints. They also leverage automatic differentiation to differentiate the neural network outputs with respect to their inputs (i.e., spatiotemporal coordinates and model parameters). By minimizing the loss function, the network can closely approximate the solution. As a result, PiNNs benefit from the long-standing achievements in mathematical physics. They are limited due to theoretical (e.g., convergence and stability) and implementation considerations (e.g., neural network design, boundary condition management, and optimization).

Let us assume that the physics of the system of interest can be described using nonlinear PDEs of the general form.

$$u_t + N[u;\lambda] = 0, t \in [0,T] \tag{6.1}$$

Here $u(t,x)$ is the solution function and $N[u,\lambda]$ is a nonlinear PDE operator with model parameters λ. This setup applies to a wide range of problems in mathematical physics, e.g., conservation laws, diffusion processes, advection–diffusion–reaction systems, kinetic equations, etc. The PiNN solution to these systems uses two NNs. The first NN is a supervised learning NN using the available but incomplete and scarce data and it approximates the true solution $u(t,x)$ under the constraint from a loss function. Let

- $\{t_u^i, x_u^i\}, (i = 1,,,N_u)$ = the time and space point values corresponding to the training data $u(t_u^i, x_u^i)$, and
- $\{u^i\}, (i = 1,,,N_u)$ = the mean values.

The loss function is chosen as the mean square error (MSE_u).

$$MSE_u = \frac{1}{N_u} \sum_{i=1}^{N_u} \left| u(t_u^i, x_u^i) - u^i \right|^2 \tag{6.2}$$

The second NN is a feed forward NN (also called multilayer perceptron or MLP) used for computing $f(t,x) = u_t + N[u; \lambda]$ on a finite set of chosen time and space point values (called *collocation* points). It transforms the input to an output through a layer of neurons using either linear maps between units in successive layers or scalar nonlinear activation functions within layers. Some of the popular activation functions are sigmoid, hyperbolic tangent, and rectified linear unit (ReLU) functions.

Let $\left\{ t_f^i, x_f^i \right\}, \left(i = 1,,, N_f \right)$ be the chosen collocation points for $f(t,x)$. They are different from the time and space points of the first NN. The corresponding loss function MSE_f is chosen as

$$\mathrm{MSE}_f = \frac{1}{N_f} \sum_{i=1}^{N_f} \left| f\left(t_f^i, x_f^i \right) \right|^2 \qquad (6.3)$$

The MSE_f enforces the structure imposed by the system PDE at the collocation points. These collocation points are added to the space and time points of the training data in the first NN. The shared parameters between the two NN are learned by minimizing the two MSEs, i.e., total $MSE = MSE_u + MSE_f$. The supervised training in the first NN now

- Includes this additional loss constraint due to physics,
- Integrates the mathematical model into the network,
- Reinforces the loss function with a residual term from the PDEs governing the system, and
- Further acts as a penalizing term to restrict the space of acceptable solutions.

Two distinct classes of algorithms have been devised using these considerations: (i) continuous time models as *data-efficient* spatiotemporal function approximators and (ii) discrete time models using implicit Runge–Kutta methods with unlimited number of temporal stages.

Some new approaches in this area use operator regression and equivariant neural network architectures with built-in physical constraints. Distributed PiNNs (DPiNNs) and distributed physics-informed extreme learning machines (DPiELMs) have been developed for approximating PDEs with strong nonlinearity or sharp gradients.

PiNNs come with several limitations and shortcomings:

- Their training may face gradient vanishing problems and can be prohibitively slow for practical three-dimensional problems. They limit low-dimensional spatiotemporal parameterization due to using fully connected layers.

- There is no theoretical proof of convergence for PiNNs when applied to problems governed by nonlinear PDEs. Additionally, all deep learning (DL) models including PiNNs generally fail to realize theoretical global minima.

- PiNNs loss function has many terms with relative weighting affecting the predicted solution.

  There are, currently, no guidelines for selecting weights optimally. Different loss function terms may compete during training, thus reducing the training process stability. PiNNs are also harder to train for an ill-posed optimization problem as they depend on soft physical constraints.

- PiNNs have bias induced by low frequency and they frequently fail to solve nonlinear PDEs for high-frequency or multiscale structures. As they learn the solutions to a given PDE for a single instance, they need a new NN to train for a new instance of the functional parameters or coefficients. This limits their generalization (e.g., spatiotemporal extrapolation). Additionally, they face difficulties in learning the solutions to inverse problems in heterogeneous media.

6.1.3 Physics-Encoded Neural Networks (PeNNs)

For situations when the explicit form of differential equations is not fully known, PeNNs are more helpful. They leverage advanced architectures to address issues with data sparsity and the lack of generalization encountered by both PgNNs and PiNNs. They can forcibly encode the known physics into their core architecture and can extend the NN's learning capability from instance learning (used by PgNNs and PiNNs) to continuous learning. Some approaches like physics-encoded recurrent convolutional neural network (PeRCNN) and neural ordinary differential equations (NeuralODE) have shown much improvement over PiNNs.

The encoding mechanisms of the underlying physics in PeNNs are fundamentally different from those in PiNNs. Additionally, both NNs can be integrated to achieve the desired nonlinearity of the model. The NNs generated by PeNNs perform better in the presence of data sparsity and poor model generalizability when compared with PgNNs and PiNNs.

The most important limitation of PeNNs occurs in training and is similar to PgNNs and PiNNs. Their architecture is also comparatively more complex. Their advantage lies in their (i) more efficient algorithms in the finite-dimensional setting, (ii) their ability to provide transferable solutions, (iii) their robustness against data scarcity, and (iv) their generalizability compared to PgNNs and PiNNs.

6.1.4 Neural Operators (NOs)

The NOs use supervised learning in a manner that is different from previous categories of PgNN, PiNN, and PeNN. They learn the underlying linear and nonlinear continuous operators (such as integrals and fractional Laplacians) by using advanced architectures (e.g., DeepONet). Their data-intensive learning resembles the PgNNs, as they both enforce the physics of the problem by using labeled input--output dataset pairs. However,

NOs are also very different from PgNNs which cannot be generalized due to under-parameterization.

NOs can be combined with PiNNs and PeNNs to train a model for learning complex nonlinearity in physical systems with extremely high generalization accuracy. They are very robust for applications requiring real-time inference. Most of the DL methods like PgNNs, PiNNs, and PeNNs generally map the solution of a physical phenomenon for a single instance (e.g., a certain spatiotemporal domain and boundary conditions to solve a PDE using PiNN), and thus must re-train or further train (e.g., transfer learning) to map the solution under a different instant. One can instead use NOs to

- Learn nonlinear mappings between function spaces and the underlying linear and nonlinear continuous operators,
- Enforce the physics of the problem using labeled input–output dataset pairs and also provide enhanced generalization, interpretability, continuous learning, and computational efficiency compared to PgNNs, PiNNs, and PeNNs, and
- Use NN-based mesh-invariant, infinite-dimensional operators that do not require a prior understanding of PDEs.

NOs work with data to learn the resolution invariant solution and can be trained on one spatiotemporal resolution and successfully inferred on any other. This resolution invariance is achieved because NOs learn continuous functions rather than discretized vectors by parameterizing the model in function spaces. They are very robust for applications requiring real-time inference. Three main NOs have been proposed recently, namely, (i) deep operator networks (DeepONets), (ii) Fourier NO (FNO), and (iii) graph NO (GNO).

6.1.5 Physics-Informed Reinforcement Learning (PiRL)

In the traditional DRL approaches, the quality and efficiency of input samples has been a major problem. Model-based RL improves on this by learning the transition dynamics and reward function of the environment to generate sample system trajectories. It then backpropagates through them to update the policy by using the differentiability of the model. This can be further improved by using a much more accurate, physics-informed neural network-based dynamics model.

One of the common approaches for implementing PiRL has three steps:

i. *Interaction with the environment*: Current policy for connecting states to actions is used to interact with the environment and gather data.

ii. *Learning the model*: The data collected in the first step is used to learn the model for system dynamics. There are two approaches for this step.

- Given the current state and action the next state is predicted by training a standard deep NN (DNN).
- In another approach the underlying Lagrangian of the model is used to derive the equations of motion from which the next state of the system is predicted.

iii. *Learning the behavior*: The model learned in the second step is used to generate imaginary trajectories.

Afterwards, the policy is updated by backpropagating through them. This is accomplished by using the physics behind the model and the differentiability of the resulting equations. In reward learning a network is trained to map the next state to the reward using the **Absolute Error Loss** (also known as L1 loss) between the predicted reward and the ground truth as the loss function.

These general ideas and methods can be adapted to study many systems and phenomena of interest with an underlying physics-based model.

6.2 TRANSFORMERS

Transformer in a neural network (NN) setting is a DL model and is generally used for sequence modeling and sequence-to-sequence prediction. Basically, it transforms one sequence of input into another depending on the problem statement. This task is also performed by other DL models like RNNs and LSTMs but unlike them the transformers process the entire sequence at once and use the mechanism of '*attention*' to weigh parts of input differently.

Recently, they have shown tremendous success in natural language processing (NLP), computer vision, and similar other tasks.

There are many variations on this simple idea resulting in different architectures.

- The original Encoder-Decoder Transformer (EDT) is a sequence-to-sequence transformer.
- Bidirectional Encoder Representations from Transformer (BERT) is an encoder-only transformer.
- Generative Pretrained Transformer (GPT) is a decoder-only transformer.

Here encoder and decoder refer to the main components of their architecture.

The basic structure of a transformer is made of many layers.

i. **Inputs:** They are the numeric representation of the sequence to be transformed. As text directly can't be used as NN input, a tokenizer is used to generate numeric representation for each token which is then sent to the encoder.

ii. **The input embedding layer:** It generates input embeddings of model dimension d_m (generally chosen as 512 but can be different) for each token.

iii. **The positional embedding layer:** It encodes information about every token t's position (denoted by *2i*).

$$(PE(t)_{2i}, PE(t)_{2i+1}) = (\sin\theta, \cos\theta), \theta = t*N^{-2i/d_{model}}$$

$$N \gg \text{the largest } k, i\,e.g., N = 10000, \forall i \in \left\{0, 1, \ldots, \frac{d_m}{2} - 1\right\}$$

The position encoding output is added to the *input embedding layer.*

iv. **The attention layer:** It uses the concept of '*attention*' to provide importance to a few key tokens *in the input sequence by altering the token embeddings. The calculation of* '*attention*' needs *the following matrices and vectors.*

- The Query, Key, and Value weight matrices are,
  - Q_w = *Query weight matrix (dimension* = $d_m X d_k$),
  - K_w = *Key weight matrix (dimension* = $d_m X d_k$), and
  - V_w = *Value weight matrix (dimension* = $d_m X d_v$).

- *The Query, Key, and Value matrices use the token matrix E (dimension* = $n\,X\,d_m$*) generated at the input embedding layer. Then for* n *tokens they are,*
  - $Q = E\,X\,Q_w$ = *Query matrix (dimension* = $n\,X\,d_k$),
  - $K = E\,X\,K_w$ = *Key matrix (dimension* = $n\,X\,d_k$), and
  - $V = E\,X\,V_w$ = *Value matrix (dimension* = $n\,X$ d_v*).Each of these matrices has* n *rows and* d_k or d_v (generally 64 but can be different) columns.

Those columns are the Query, Key, and Value vectors belonging to the corresponding matrices.

These matrices are derived from the linear transformations of the input sequence as described above. Typically, Q corresponds to the current element, K represents other elements, and V encapsulates information to be aggregated.

*Then the '**attention**' for each token **n** is defined as*

$$\left[Attention(Q,K,V) \right]_n = \left[softmax\left(QK^T / \sqrt{d_k} \right)V \right]_n \quad (6.4)$$

By definition, $softmax(z_i) = \dfrac{e^{z_i}}{\sum_{i=1}^{K} e^{z_i}}$. The attention is calculated for each token.

The basic idea behind '*attention*' assumes that given an input text, it is possible to allocate distinct weights to individual words to capture dependencies and contextual relationships within the sequence. Each element within the sequence has its unique representation.

The association weight between the current element and others is determined by calculating the similarity between the Q and K matrices through their dot product normalized using the softmax function. The normalized weights are then applied to the corresponding values, followed by their aggregation. This results in a representation encompassing the association between the current word and other words in the text and is formally expressed as 'attention' given above.

v. **The multi-head attention layer:** It is a **stack of parallel attention layers** with **n x d_m dimension**. It helps in understanding different aspects of a sequence (e.g., sentence or a language). Each head in this layer takes in the positional encoding generated earlier and produces an output of shape **n x d_k each.** This output from all heads is then concatenated to produce a single output of the dimension **n x d_m.** LSTM or RNN cannot be used for this purpose as they may lack sufficient memory for complex tasks like Language Translation.

vi. **Generative pretrained transformer and ChatGPT**

There are two core techniques behind this new and revolutionary application which has brought AI to everyone's attention.

i. *Transformer as the backbone architecture*: It has become an essential foundation for the recent development of large language models, such as BERT and GPT. Transformer idea has also been extended from language to visuals, so that it has become a unified backbone architecture for both NLP and computer vision.

ii. *Autoregressive Generative Pretraining*: These methods have become the foundation of GPT models as they handle the statistical analysis of time series data very well. These models specify that the output variable is linearly dependent on its preceding values. For NLP, they predict the subsequent word given the previous word, or the last probable word given the following words. The models learn a joint distribution of sequence data, employing previous time steps as inputs to forecast each variable in the sequence. The joint distribution $p_\theta(x)$ can be factorized into a product of conditional distributions, as demonstrated below:

$$p_\theta(x) = p_\theta(x_1) p_\theta(x_2|x_1) \ldots p_\theta(x_n|x_1, x_2, \ldots, x_{n-1}) \quad (6.5)$$

The RNNs are architecturally similar, and they use the previous hidden state but autoregressive models use previous time steps as input. They are like a feed-forward network that incorporates all preceding time-step variables as inputs. Recently, the autoregressive approach has been extended to continuous variables as well.

6.3 GENERATIVE AI

Generative AI (GAI) is a type of AI which learns the patterns and structures of the input data in one media in detail and then generates output data of different types of media (e.g., text, images, etc.) when prompted. Traditional AI focusses on detecting patterns, making decisions, improving analytics, classifying data, etc. using CNN, RNN, RL, etc. GAI produces new contents, responses, synthetic data, etc., using Transformers, GANs, and variable auto-encoders. The recent excitement about GAI is due to the simplicity of its user interfaces.

The GANs, transformers, and large language models allowed the GAI to take off even though this technical approach was first used in 1960s chatbots. Especially, transformers made it possible to train ever-larger models, e.g., billions of pages of text, without labeling all the data in advance. This resulted in answers with more depth using the idea of '*attention*' to track the connections between words across pages, chapters, and books and connections to analyze codes, proteins, chemicals, DNA, etc. Further innovations in multimodal AI allowed content generation across the media, e.g., images from text, etc. Basic *generative model* denoted by P_{model} has the following properties:

- Given a dataset of observations X generated according to an unknown distribution P_{data}, the P_{model} can mimic P_{data}.
- By sampling from P_{model}, observations that appear to have been drawn from P_{data} can be generated.
- Generative DL consists in applying DL techniques to learn P_{model}.

Table 6.2 summarizes these points.
The GAI can use DRL methods to increase its capabilities with three types of applications as shown in the table above.

6.3.1 Model Generation without Specified Objectives

RL is especially useful for deriving generative models for non-differentiable losses, e.g., GANs can be used for text-generation for which traditional techniques are not suitable. It can also be applied to domains in which feasibility and correctness (e.g., running code as above) are very essential. RL can produce observations that appear to have been drawn from the domain of interest even when such domain cannot be modeled by means of generative functions and corresponding differentiable losses. It can also derive more complex generative strategies (e.g., through hierarchical RL) and reduce the model dependence on training data.

There are some limitations of this approach as learning without supervision is a hard task, when the reward is sparse, e.g., sequence generation of long text or music, where the reward is available only at the last timestep. In addition to the techniques for obtaining a denser reward, a potential solution might be an intrinsic reward. Ensuring a sufficient exploration of all possible actions while still exploiting the most promising ones to collect higher rewards is one of the key problems in RL.

6.3.2 Generation of Outputs While Concurrently Maximizing an Objective Function

RL for objective maximization can consider generators adapted for domains or for specific problems, or for tasks difficult to model through differentiable functions. Also, pretrained models can be fine-tuned to given requirements and specifications. The goal is to derive *the best possible examples* according to some specific target functions. Any desired and quantifiable property can be Reward Function. Apart from text or music generation, other domains might be considered as well.

TABLE 6.2   DRL in GAI

Goal	Reward	Advantages	Limitations
Mere generation	• GAN's discriminative signal • Log-likelihood of realor predicted targets • Constraint satisfaction	• Model domains have nondifferentiable objectives • Adapts GAN to sequential tasks • Can implement RL strategies, e.g., hierarchical RL	• No supervision learning is hard • Pretraining can prevent an appropriate exploration
Objective maximization	• Test-time metrics • Countable desiredorundesired characteristics • Distance-based measures • Quantifiable properties • Output of ML algorithms	• Quantifiable requirements satisfied • Generator from a specific domain toward desirable sub-domains optimized • Gap between training and evaluation reduced	• Not every desirable property is quantifiable
Improving not easily quantifiable characteristics	Output of a model trained to reproduce human or AI feedback about non-quantifiable properties (e.g., helpfulness, appropriateness, creativity, etc.)	• Satisfies nonquantifiable requirements, e.g., the alignment problem • Requires preferences between candidates instead of defining a mathematical measure of desired property	• Getting user preferences expensive • Users may misbehave, disagree, or be biased • Reward modeling is difficult • Prone to jailbreaks out of alignment

Source   Reinforcement Learning for Generative AI: State of the Art, Opportunities and Open Research Challenges, by Giorgio Franceschelli and Mirco Musolesi, arXiv:2308.00031v4 [cs.LG] 8 Feb 2024.

There are some drawbacks of this approach like its very high computational cost due to the number of iterations required for convergence. In addition, certain desired properties (e.g. harmlessness or appropriateness) can be difficult to quantify. New metrics are then required, and a gap between training objective and test score might be inevitable.

6.3.3 Embedding of Desired Characteristics, Which Cannot be Easily Captured by Means of an Objective Function, into the Generative Process

Reward modeling introduces a great level of flexibility in RL for GAI. Generative models can be trained to produce content with appropriate and of sufficient quality, by aligning them with human preferences. It becomes essential when a quantifiable measure might not exist or information to derive it might be hard to obtain.

Sometimes reward modeling may lead to reduction of the diversity to a single reward function. This may cause the majority views to disproportionately prevail. In addition, seemingly well-performing preference-based reward models might fail to generalize. More advanced approaches may be required to mitigate this problem and completely prevent certain undesired behaviors.

6.4 EXPLAINABLE AI AND RL

Explainable AI (XAI) is a type of AI with an architecture such that the reasoning behind its decision can be understood or explained. In traditional AI, the inner mechanism of the NN is like a blackbox that can answer 'yes' or 'no' type questions but the reasoning behind it is mostly untraceable. There are many situations e.g., in legal and medical field, where answers to other '*wh*' questions (such as 'why,' 'when,' 'where, etc.) are needed but usual AI cannot answer them. XAI considerations and methods should be able to handle the following concerns.

(i) Transparency
This is provided if XAI justifications are such that minimally a human should be able to understand it. In its absence situations can arise in which a false training can be used to tweak any AI/ML model to providing unethical benefits to an interested party.

(ii) Trust and confidence
Trust is essential if humans have to rely on any AI/ML outcome. A logical and scientific justification for any prediction and conclusion should be available.

(iii) Bias and fairness
There is a trade-off between bias and variance in AI/ML models. It must be handled so that bias is reduced, and one can believe the predictions of the model.

The XAI aims to provide an understanding of how AI models work and reasons beyond the decisions they make, allowing users to understand their results. This is particularly important as AI becomes more integrated into everyday life and critical decision-making processes such as healthcare and finance. The XAI explanations should also improve the AI model performance based on understanding its decision-making strategies so that explanations about the model outputs can help tune the ML system parameters better. For the DNN-based XAI building an explanation is challenging for two reasons: (i) DNNs offer excellent performances at the price of high inner complexity of the models and (ii) the explanations should be humanly understandable, which many times are unavailable.

The XAI techniques can be divided into two broad categories:

 i. *Transparent methods*, e.g., logistic regression, support vector machine (SVM), Bayesian classifier, K-nearest-neighbors (KNN), decision trees (DT), rule-based learning (simple conditional if-else form or first-order predictive logic), and fuzzy inference systems are simple to represent and interpret. They are more useful when internal feature correlations are less complex. There are three main approaches to transparency.

- Simulatability implies that the model must be human-executable, e.g., sparse matrix model is easier to interpret than dense matrix one as it is easy to justify and visualize by humans.

- Decomposability means that each aspect of the model from input of data to hyperparameters and inherent calculations should be easy to understand.

- Algorithmic transparency defines algorithm level interpretability from input of given data to final decision or classification. With the help of visualization users can understand how the model reacts to different situations.

ii. *Post-hoc methods* work better for data with nonlinear relationship or higher complexity. After receiving a trained and/or tested AI model as input, such methods generate useful approximations of the model's inner working and decision logic as feature importance scores, rule sets, heat maps, or natural language. They are further classified into model agnostic and model-specific methods.

- Model-agnostic explanations observe the change in output after perturbing the samples. Then they extract feature importance scores and build a simplified local model that approximates the original model's behavior near the original samples. These tools use pairwise analysis and can be used for any AI/ML model.

- Model-specific techniques find explanations specific to the given algorithm and relevant to the internal structure of the learning model, such as (i) finding the impact factors and correlations of the most important features, (ii) condition-based explanations answering 'why' questions, and (iii) finding simple rules capturing the complex input–output relations of the given model.

6.4.1 Explainable RL

The impressive performance and remarkable recent achievements of RL systems can be attributed to combining RL with DL. However, explainability, which refers to the understanding of the system's decision-making process, is lacking. In response to this challenge, the new explainable RL (XRL) field has emerged and is growing rapidly to help us understand the RL systems.

The XAI focuses on many forms of learning like unsupervised and supervised learning. In supervised learning, observations are assumed to be independent and identically distributed and the goal is to minimize the risk with immediate response. In contrast, the agent in RL learns to maximize the return with rewards as the responses, which are not necessarily provided immediately. Hence, the agent needs to consider the short-term and long-term consequences in addition to the immediate response when learning to make decisions. Accordingly, methods to explain these RL-specific characteristics are different from XAI.

The following considerations are very important for XRL.

i. *Trust*: One way to understand trust is whether a stakeholder is willing to delegate the decision-making to the AI system. Thus, if one is inclined to let the AI system decide on its behalf, then it trusts the system. Also, trust can be the confidence that the system will behave as intended.

ii. *New insight*: This is the ability to extract knowledge from the AI system to gain a new understanding of the problem at hand. Creating an RL system is not only for making decisions but also for gaining novel insights into the domain.

iii. *Making adjustments*: It should be possible to change an AI system for correcting and improving it. Different quantities, such as accuracy and return indicate the system's performance but lack the ability to find, fix, and improve it. Hence, knowing how the system works, and also its strengths and weaknesses is required to find bugs, fix them, determine when the system might fail, and improve it.

iv. *Fairness and being ethical*: These ensure that the AI system does not make decisions that, for example, might discriminate based on skin color or gender and complies with ethical standards.

Apart from these reasons, there are others like effective human and AI collaboration, privacy, and accountability that motivate the need for explainability.

6.5 GRAPH NEURAL NETWORKS (GNNS)

GNNs are evolutions of CNNs and graph embedding. They can work with usually highly complex data structures given as a graph, e.g., a grid of pixels, to predict a class. Like Recurrence NN used in text classification, the GNNs are applied to graph structures where every word is a node in a sentence. They were introduced when CNNs were applied to complex graphs with arbitrarily large sizes but failed to achieve optimal results. They are particularly used in pattern recognition, social networks analysis, recommendation systems, and semantic analysis.

In general, GNNs are used in predicting nodes, edges, and graph-based tasks. A node can be a person, place, or thing, connected with the edges defining the relationships between them. The edges can be directed and undirected based on directional dependencies. In general graphs exist in non-Euclidean spaces which sometimes makes it harder to interpret them.

Some of the types of GNN are the following.

- **Graph Convolutional Networks (GCNs): They** are like traditional CNNs containing graph convolution, linear layer, and non-learner activation function. There are two major types Spatial GCNs and Spectral GCNs.

- **Graph Auto-Encoder Networks (GAENNs):** They learn graph representation using an encoder and attempt to reconstruct input graphs using a decoder. The encoder and decoders are joined by a bottleneck layer.

- **Recurrent Graph Neural Networks (RGNNs):** They are good with multi-relational graphs where a single node has multiple relations. They use regularizers to boost smoothness and eliminate over-parameterization. RGNNs use less computation power to produce better results. They are used in generating text, machine translation, speech recognition, generating image descriptions, video tagging, and text summarization.

- **Gated Graph Neural Networks (GGNNs):** They are better than the RGNNs in performing tasks with long-term dependencies. Like GRUs, they use gates to remember and forget information in different states.

6.5.1 GNN and DRL

State-of-the-art DRL-based networking solutions use standard NN. e.g., fully connected, convolutional, etc., which are usually unable to learn from information structured as graphs.

One of the solutions proposed to mitigate this problem is to relate Q-function to the graph metrics of the GNN. The GNN-based DRL agent defines the actions to apply on the network topology. The actions allocate the demands on one of the candidate paths. The DRL agent implements the DQN algorithm, where the Q-function is modeled by a GNN. At the same time, the environment (i) defines the optimization problem to solve, (ii) stores the network topology, together with the link features, (iii) generates the reward once an action is performed.

In the iterative learning process, the agent receives a graph-structured network state observation from the environment.

The GNN constructs a graph representation with topology links as the graph entities. An iterative message-passing algorithm running between the links' hidden states outputs a global hidden state encoding the topology and processed by a DNN. At the end of this phase, the GNN outputs a Q-function estimate. This is evaluated over a limited set of actions, and finally the DRL agent selects the action with the highest Q-value. Application of DRL in GNN is still a very active research area.

6.6 BINARIZED NNS (BNN)

Regular NNs need powerful GPUs for training. Even after quantization the NN weights have *int8* precision, which makes training and inference still very compute-intensive and not very energy-cost-friendly. The BNN is a new type of neural network which stores weights in binary values, i.e., 1 and –1, also known as 1-bit quantization. This uses just 1 bit for weights and/or activations instead of full precision values and substitutes complex multiply-accumulate operations with bitwise logic operations. Thus, computation and memory footprint are reduced drastically so that they become very suitable for embedded devices and microcontrollers.

6.7 REINFORCEMENT LEARNING FROM HUMAN FEEDBACK (RLHF)

In usual DRL approach, the agent learns the policy giving the optimal reward function by trial-and-error iterations. However, explicitly defining a reward function that accurately approximates human preferences is challenging. RLHF is a technique for aligning an intelligent agent with human preferences. In this approach, first a reward model is trained in a supervised manner to represent human preferences directly. This reward function is then used to improve an agent's policy through an optimization algorithm like proximal policy optimization (PPO).

The algorithm was introduced by OpenAI for enhancing text continuation or summarization based on human feedback; later it was reused in InstructGPT. RLHF has been applied to many areas of machine learning, e.g., text summarization, conversational agents, text-to-image models, etc. One of the problems with RLHF is the high cost of acquiring high-quality preference data without any biases.

6.8 QUANTUM RL

First we have to understand the basis of quantum computing using some basic concepts of quantum mechanics.

6.8.1 Single and Multi-Qubit Systems

The basic unit of classical information is a single bit which can be either in state 0 or in state 1. A sequence of n such bits can represent 2^n unique values and the bit register can only be in one of these 2^n states at any point in time. On the other hand, the basic unit of quantum information is a single qubit with $|0\rangle$ and $|1\rangle$ as its two distinct, orthogonal states. These *basis states* span a two-dimensional Hilbert space, which contains all 1-qubit (pure) quantum states. The qubits can be realized physically in many ways, e.g., spin systems of subatomic particles, ion traps, neutral atoms, or superconducting circuits. An arbitrary qubit can not only be in $|0\rangle$ and $|1\rangle$ states but also be in a *superposition* of both.

$$|\Psi\rangle = A\,|0\rangle + B\,|1\rangle \qquad (6.6)$$

The *amplitudes* α and β are complex numbers satisfying $|\alpha|^2 + |\beta|^2 = 1$. Alternatively, one can write

$$|\psi\rangle = \left(cos\frac{\theta}{2}|0\rangle + e^{i\phi}sin\frac{\theta}{2}|1\rangle\right) \qquad (6.7)$$

This representation makes it possible to visualize the state of a 1-qubit system on the surface of the *Bloch sphere*, in which the north and south poles on the z-axis correspond to the basis states |0> and |>1. They are the *computational basis states* of a single qubit. Alternatively, qubits can be represented in other ways also.

- By the poles related to the x-axis

$$|+\rangle = \frac{|0\rangle + |1\rangle}{\sqrt{2}}, |-\rangle = \frac{|0\rangle - |1\rangle}{\sqrt{2}} \quad (6.8)$$

- By a complex combination

$$|R\rangle = \frac{|0\rangle + i|1\rangle}{\sqrt{2}}, |L\rangle = \frac{|0\rangle - i|1\rangle}{\sqrt{2}} \quad (6.9)$$

- By a column vector

$$|0\rangle \rightarrow \begin{bmatrix} 1 \\ 0 \end{bmatrix}, |1\rangle \rightarrow \begin{bmatrix} 0 \\ 1 \end{bmatrix}$$

An n-qubit system gives access to the 2^n-dimensional Hilbert space, in which an arbitrary *pure* quantum state is given as

$$|\psi\rangle = c_0 |00\cdots00\rangle + c_1 |00\cdots01\rangle + \cdots + c_{2^n-1} |11\cdots11\rangle \quad (6.10)$$

The basis states consist of tensor products of the individual qubits. The state $|\psi\rangle$ has 2^n complex amplitudes, whose absolute squared values must sum up to 1. Due to the principle of superposition, an n-qubit system can encode and process information scaling in O (2^n), while for a classical setting, it is limited to O (n).

6.8.1.1 Evolution of Closed Quantum Systems

The quantum computation is achieved by *operators* acting on the Hilbert space. They describe the time evolution of a closed quantum system and are reversible, so they can be represented as unitary matrices, i.e., for an operator U it must hold that $U^\dagger U = I$. This constraint preserves the length. The operators are:

$$X := \sigma_x = \begin{bmatrix} 0 & 1 \\ 1 & 0 \end{bmatrix}, Y := \sigma_y = \begin{bmatrix} 0 & -i \\ i & 0 \end{bmatrix}, Z := \sigma_z = \begin{bmatrix} 1 & 0 \\ 0 & -1 \end{bmatrix}$$

(6.11)

The operator for arbitrary rotation with θ about axis i as

$$R_i(\theta) = e^{-i\frac{\theta}{2}\sigma_i}$$ (6.12)

The last 1-qubit operator is the *Hadamard* matrix:

$$H := \frac{1}{\sqrt{2}} \begin{bmatrix} 1 & 1 \\ 1 & -1 \end{bmatrix}$$ (6.13)

The 1-qubit operators can be extended to act a multi-qubit system. For example, the most relevant 2-qubit operators are the controlled X (CX) and controlled Z (CZ), where one qubit acts as the control and the other acts as the target. Similarly, the CX-gate flips the amplitudes of the target qubit and the CZ operator performs a conditional phase flip.

6.8.1.2 Extracting Classical Information via Measurements

For quantum systems, in order to extract information, an *observable* quantity has to be measured, which is a Hermitian operator O such that $O^\dagger = O$. The eigenstates of O define a basis of the quantum system's Hilbert space.

After measuring an observable O, the device outputs an eigenvalue of O and the system is in the corresponding eigenstate. Let $|0\rangle$, $|1\rangle$, ..., $|N - 1\rangle$ be the basis defined by observable O and c_0, c_1, ..., c_N the corresponding amplitudes of state $|\psi\rangle$ expressed in this basis. Then measuring O gives the outcome λ_i with probability $|c_i|^2$. Consequently, having obtained λ_i, the post-measurement state of the system is $|i\rangle$. The quantum circuits represent the measurement process with quantum circuit diagrams as the computing steps of a quantum algorithm. The diagrams give its sequence of operators, states, and measurement.

6.8.2 Quantum RL (QRL)

It is the study and application of quantum ML (QML) as described above to RL tasks. QML integrates quantum algorithms with ML programs mostly for the classical data used in quantum computing. Qubits (and in principle Qudits) with relevant quantum operations are used to improve the computational speed and data storage. In general, QRL handles computationally difficult subroutines. Most of them take one of the following approaches.

- Quantum-inspired RL algorithms, e.g., amplitude amplification-based action selection
- Variable quantum circuits (VQCs)-based function approximation for actor, critic, MARL, etc.
- RL algorithms with quantum subroutines, e.g., quantum policy or value iteration, projective simulation, Boltzmann machines for function approximation, etc.
- Full QRL, e.g., quantum policy iteration, quantum gradient estimation, etc.

6.8.3 Variational Quantum Circuits

The VQCs combine the strength of both classical and quantum computation. They use quantum circuits with tunable parameters on noisy intermediate-scale quantum (NISQ) hardware optimizing them iteratively on a classical computer. Those parameters then become weights in an artificial NN. The DRL combined with NISQ computation is an RL agent interacting with the environment. It then gains knowledge of backgrounds and derives the policy for making the optimal decision.

The VQC can model any function approximators, classifiers, and even quantum-many body physics that are intractable on classical computers. Even without any quantum error correction, or fault-tolerant quantum computation, they have been shown to avoid the complex quantum errors existing in other quantum devices. Just like classical NN, they can approximate any analytic action-value function of DRL.

The foundations of QC, and by implication QML, were established with the development of the theory of quantum physics in the early 20th century. Feynman had proposed the idea of taking advantage of quantum mechanics for computing in the early 1980s. QC potentially provides efficient solutions to classically intractable problems

6.8.4 Quantum RL Algorithms

Most often, RL is used to:

- Generate a solution for a quantum control problem, e.g., to learn quantum error correction strategies or to generate control policies at a lower error rate.
- Optimize a variational quantum algorithm (VQA).
- Optimize supervised and unsupervised learning.
- Employ VQCs as function approximators.

In the method of amplitude amplification, as it is used in Grover-type search algorithms, several qubit registers embed the states and actions relevant for the RL system in a suitable Hilbert space. Starting from a uniform superposition, amplitudes favored by the reward or the value function are selectively amplified based on Born's rule, i.e., a measurement is carried out on the qubit register with regard to the 'action-basis.'

Projective Simulation (PS): Another QRL method is based on PS, which in the broadest sense is a particular learning paradigm and similar in spirit to RL. Based on experiences made through interaction with the environment, a memory network is created by the agent. The network has a directed structure with adaptive weights between the nodes of the network. The learning process and action selection are based on a random process (more precisely, a random walk) on the graph of the network, with the transition probabilities between nodes being given by the respective adaptive weights. PS can be 'quantized' by replacing the random walk with a so-called quantum random walk. Possible quantum advantages over classical PS lie in the acceleration of the process of action selection.

Quantum Boltzmann Machines: Boltzmann machines are used as function approximators. These models are assumed to be advantageous compared to typical NNs in environments with large action spaces. Boltzmann machines are closely related to energy-based models. For specific instances, those allow for a quantum representation, which enables potential quantum speed-up for post-NISQ devices.

Quantum Subroutines: Another approach to go from RL to QRL replaces certain subroutines in existing RL approaches. One idea is to replace policy or value iteration with some quantum-enhanced analogs. While this approach is limited to universal, fault-tolerant and error-corrected quantum hardware, several such algorithms have been proposed.

CHAPTER 7

Applications of RL

A S EVERYDAY NEWS CONFIRMS, AI/ML has emerged as a
revolutionary technology applied in practically every area
of human endeavor. In many situations it has solved problems
deemed insoluble using standard techniques of analytical
modeling and computational programming. In this chapter
we will try to give a glimpse of the depth and breadth of these
applications focused on RL.

7.1 SELF-DRIVING CARS

RL agents applied to traffic pattern can learn traffic density,
vehicle flow patterns, speed, etc., in real time and continuously.
They can then adapt the system in the preferred direction and
keep repeating this in real time to make traffic safer and its flow
smoother across times, climates, and seasons.

DOI: 10.1201/9781032659800-7

RL is behind the related new technology of self-driving cars which promises to revolutionize personal transportation. The DRL network trains self-driving cars by using sensor data feedback collected during driving sessions in varied and unfamiliar terrains. This way they learn and avoid accidents anywhere in principle. Some cities on the west coast have allowed them on the roads, which is a sign of the maturity of this approach.

Autonomous driving (AD) systems contain many perception-level tasks for which high precision has been achieved using DRL. In addition to perception, AD systems must deal with other tasks for which classical supervised learning methods are not applicable.

(i) The prediction of the agent's action changes future sensor observations received from the environment, e.g., determining the optimal driving speed in an urban area.

(ii) Supervisory signals such as time to collision (TTC) and lateral error w.r.t. [sic] to optimal trajectory of the agent, represent the dynamics of the agent, as well [as] uncertainty in the environment. Such problems require defining the stochastic cost function to be maximized.

(iii) The agent is required to learn new configurations of the environment and predict an optimal decision at each instant while driving. This represents a high-dimensional space given the number of unique configurations under which the agent and environment are observed.

In all such scenarios RL methods provide the best approach to an optimized solution to the problems outlined above. AD tasks where RL could be applied include the following:

- Controller optimization
- Path planning and trajectory optimization
- Motion planning and dynamic path planning

- Development of high-level driving policies for complex navigation tasks
- Scenario-based policy learning for highways, intersections, merges and splits
- Reward learning with inverse RL from expert data for intent prediction of traffic actors such as pedestrian and vehicles
- Learning of policies for ensuring safety and performing risk estimation.

Before discussing the applications of DRL to AD tasks we briefly review the state space, action space, and rewards schemes in AD setting.

7.1.1 State Spaces, Action Spaces, and Rewards

Commonly used state space features for an autonomous vehicle under consideration (called ego-vehicle) include the following:

i. Position, heading, and velocity of ego-vehicle.

ii. Same for other obstacles in the sensor view of the ego-vehicle. To avoid variations in the dimension of the state space, a Cartesian or Polar occupancy grid around the ego vehicle is used.

iii. Lane information such as lane number (ego-lane or others).

iv. Path curvature.

v. Past and future trajectory of the ego-vehicle.

vi. Longitudinal information such as time-to-collision (TTC)

vii. Scene information such as traffic laws and signal locations.

AD uses the following kinds of data:

i. Raw sensor data such as camera images, LiDAR, radar, etc., for finer contextual information.

ii. Condensed abstracted data for reducing the complexity of the state space.

iii. In between data or a mid-level representation such as 2D bird's-eye view. It is sensor agnostic but still close to the spatial organization of the scene, retaining the spatial layout of roads which graph-based representations cannot do.

A vehicle policy must control several continuous-valued actuators, e.g., steering angle, throttle, and brake, and discrete-valued ones controlling gear changes. The continuous action space can be discretized uniformly by dividing the range of continuous actuators (such as steering angle, throttle, and brake) into equal sized bins. Discretization has to be done carefully as it can lead to jerky or unstable trajectories if the step values between actions are too large. There is also a trade-off between having enough discrete steps to allow for smooth control and not having so many steps that action selections become prohibitively expensive to evaluate. As an alternative, continuous values for actuators may also be handled by DRL algorithms which learn a policy directly (e.g. DDPG). Designing reward functions for DRL agents for autonomous driving is still very much an open question, but many approaches are becoming available.

7.1.2 Motion Planning and Trajectory Optimization

Motion planning ensures the existence of a path between target and destination. Path planning in dynamic environments and varying vehicle dynamics is a key AD problem, e.g., negotiating right to pass through in an intersection, merging into highways, etc. The DDPG algorithm has been found quite useful in handling these situations. Classical RL methods are used to perform optimal control in stochastic settings, e.g., the Linear Quadratic

Regulator (LQR) in linear regimes and iterative LQR (iLQR) for nonlinear regimes are utilized.

7.1.3 Simulator and Scenario Generation Tools

AD datasets address supervised learning setup with training sets containing image, label pairs for various modalities. RL requires an environment where state-action pairs can be recovered while modeling dynamics of the vehicle state, environment, as well as the stochasticity in the movement and actions of the environment and agent, respectively. Various simulators have been developed for this purpose.

7.1.4 Learn from Demonstrations (LfD) and Inverse Reinforcement Learning (IRL) for AD Applications

LfD agent mimics the behavior of an expert. Sometimes a CNN is trained to map raw pixels from a single front-facing camera directly to steering commands. Using a relatively small training dataset from humans/experts, the system learns to drive in traffic on local roads with or without lane markings and on highways. The network learns image representations that detect the road successfully, without being explicitly trained to do so. Maximum entropy inverse RL is one of the methods used for this purpose.

7.2 VIDEO GAMES

Video games have long been of great interest to AI researchers, especially Atari games which are used to test control problems. The use of AI in its design has made the games better in the way people play them. The researchers are now trying to achieving super-human-level performance in playing them. The application of DRL enables agents to learn making decisions in high-dimensional environments and it has brought many developments in this area.

Example: Atari Game – Pong

The environment consists of

- Two solid rebounding walls at the top and bottom
- Two agents represented by paddles and a ball.

The actions that the agent can perform are:

- Move up or
- Move down.

The objective is to keep shuttling the ball without letting it touch the leftmost and rightmost walls. Every time an agent fails to prevent the ball from touching the side walls, a penalty is levied. Training needs to be done to aid the agent in decision-making – to either go up or go down.

In a supervised learning approach, a label needs to be given to every sequence of actions. This is very problematic:

1. The human controlling the agent must be highly skilled in order to get high performance rates.
2. The dataset created must be large enough to cover all possible action sequences.
3. Since the model is trained on a dataset created by a human, the performance can at best be equal to him/her.

So supervised learning cannot be used to perform better than humans.

DRL overcomes these problems. Its framework is very similar to that of supervised learning. There is an input frame, a neural network, and an output action, the difference being that there is no target label in DRL. Policy network trained using policy gradient has been found the most useful. They consider a random network which takes a high-dimensional image frame from the game engine as an input. This produces a random output action – either up or down which is sent back to the network which then produces the next frame. After every single choice, the game simulator executes the action and gives a reward as feedback. If an agent wins, a reward of +1 is given; if it loses, a penalty of –1 is given, else 0.

The goal of this entire setting is to maximize the reward obtained and make the agent learn the most appropriate decision at a given stage. In the policy gradient solution, the credit assignment problem must be solved. The entire sequence of actions should not be discarded because of a negative penalty at the end. It might be the case that the intermediate steps were beneficial and some of the later steps were not.

The importance of DRL and policy gradient solution is observed in a sparse reward setting like the game 'Montezuma's revenge.' The game environment and action sequences can be so complex that the number of sequences leading to the goal is very small. The agent will have limited positive examples to follow if it takes up random exploration. To overcome this problem, reward shaping is used. Reward shaping refers to the process of creating a reward function that is designed manually to direct the policy toward a specific behavior. However, reward shaping is not an optimal approach. The DRL approach to video games has led to impressive results in control problems.

7.3 HEALTHCARE

RL-related models and approaches have been widely applied in healthcare domains for some time now. In the early days the focus was on applying dynamic programming to develop pharmacokinetic/ pharmacodynamic models. With the tremendous theoretical and technical achievements in generalization, representation, and efficiency in recent years, RL approaches have been successfully applied in a number of healthcare domains as well. Broadly, they have been applied to three domains:

i. Dynamic treatment regimes in chronic diseases and critical care

ii. Automated medical diagnosis

iii. Others such as health resources allocation and scheduling, optimal process control, drug discovery and development, as well as health management.

7.3.1 Dynamic Treatment Regimes (DTR)

One of the goals of healthcare decision-making is to develop effective treatment regimes that can dynamically adapt to the varying clinical states and improve the long-term benefits of patients. DTR provide a new paradigm to automate the process of developing new effective treatment regimes for individual patients with long-term care.

RL in healthcare has been used in automated medical diagnosis, resource scheduling, drug discovery and development, health management, etc. It has also helped in creating DTR. It works as follows:

- The data based on the current clinical observations and assessments of the patient is entered into the DTR system.
- The DTR system already has the previous medical history data of the patient. Using RL agent, it then outputs a suggestion on treatment type, drug dosages, and appointment timing for every stage of the patient's journey to full recovery. It helps in making time-dependent decisions for the best treatment for a patient at a specific time.

Using DTR, medical professionals can save time, energy, and efforts needed to consult with multiple parties. It contains a sequence of decision rules to determine the course of actions (e.g., treatment type, drug dosage, or reexamination timing) at a time point according to the current health status and prior treatment history of an individual patient. They are tailored for generating new scientific hypotheses and developing optimal treatments across or within groups of patients. Utilizing data generated from the Sequential Multiple Assignment Randomized Trial (SMART), a DTR can be derived to optimize the final clinical outcome of particular interest. Some relations are as follows:

   i. The series of decision rules in DTRs are equivalent to the policies in RL.

  ii. The treatment outcomes are expressed by the reward functions.

 iii. The inputs in DTRs are a set of clinical observations and assessments of patients.

  iv. The outputs are the treatments options at each stage, equivalent to the states and actions in RL, respectively.

RL can achieve time-dependent decisions on the best treatment for each patient at each decision time, thus accounting for heterogeneity across patients. This precise treatment does not rely on the identification of any accurate mathematical models or explicit relationship between treatments and outcomes. These solutions improve the long-term outcomes by considering delayed effect of treatments, which is the major characteristic of medical treatment. Finally, by careful engineering of the reward function using expert or domain knowledge, RL provides an elegant way to multi-objective optimization of treatment between efficacy and the raised side effect.

The domains of applying RL in DTRs can be classified into two main categories: chronic diseases and critical care.

7.3.2 Chronic Diseases

Chronic diseases, e.g., diabetes, hypertension, schizophrenia, etc., are big public health issues worldwide, claiming a considerable portion of death every year. They last a long period of three months or more and require continuous clinical observation and medical care. Their long-term treatment contains a sequence of medical intervention that must consider the changing health status of a patient and adverse effects occurring from previous treatment. In general, the relationship of treatment duration, dosage, and type against the patient's response is too complex to be explicitly specified. RL has been utilized to automate the discovery and generation of optimal DTRs in a variety of chronic diseases including cancer, diabetes, anemia, HIV, and several common mental illnesses.

7.3.3 Critical Care

Critical care is for more seriously ill or injured patients needing special medical treatments and nursing care. Usually, these patients require intensive care unit (ICU) for intensive monitoring and close attention. They may also need sedation, nutrition, blood product administration, fluid and vasoactive drug therapy, hemodynamic endpoints, glucose control, and mechanical ventilation.

Much effort has been made in developing guidelines and standardization of the various aspects of ICU interventions. It is now possible to generate rich ICU data in a variety of formats for the applications of RL in critical care. However, the inherent 3C (compartmentalization, corruption, and complexity) features indicate that critical care data are usually noisy, biased, and incomplete.

7.4 MARKETING AND ADVERTISING

The capitalist economy is centered on increasing profits by stimulating consumption and using natural and human resources to make products and services for that purpose. Marketing and advertising are backbones of this approach. The ML approach here works as follows.

i. *Real-time advertising to target audiences*

Real-time bidding platforms, A/B testing, and automatic ad optimization are the methods used for this purpose. A series of advertisements is placed in the marketplace. The DNN-based host automatically serves the best-performing ads in the best spots for the lowest prices. The marketing and advertising platforms learn in real time the most effective ads and display them more frequently and prominently.

The same platforms use RL to associate similar companies, products, and services to prioritize for certain customers. The choice is reinforced if the consumer clicks or uses other signals of engagement, so the same strategy is repeated. The ads consumers receive are usually from companies with websites previously visited, or bought from before, or situated in the same industry as a company from which a previous purchase was made.

ii. *Recommendation systems*

The DRL systems and learning machines are further used to generate recommendation shown as tabs like 'Frequently Bought Together,' 'Customers Also Liked,' 'Recommended Reading,' etc. On news websites, they queue the next story, articles, etc., to the customer based on his/her previous preferences. They analyze customers' behavior in real time and also generate rewards to keep them engaged and interested.

A variation on this application is used to improve video streaming, e.g., Netflix. RL is used to improve the performance of its algorithms that determine which video to play next. Recommendations for new titles are made based on past choices. It starts with an initial guess about what movie the user will like based on his/her previous viewing habits. Then it recommends something new with the same or better rating. If the user selects it, then the rating specific to that user is changed for future interaction.

These systems have a dark side which is not good for encouraging critical thinking as they reward impulsive behavior based on emotions. Their use on news websites and social media has exacerbated the social fragmentation and entrenched the ideological divisions. The society at large may have to revisit these issues in future.

7.5 IMAGE AND PATTERN RECOGNITION

This is one of the most important uses of RL as it is used in both regular and security settings. RL agents can start with a given image and then identify objects sequentially until individual items in the total image are cataloged. Artificial vision systems also use deep convolution NNs with large, labeled datasets as inputs and map images to human-generated scene descriptions from simulation engines.

Some more examples of RL in image processing include the following:

- Robots with visual sensors learning from their surrounding environment.
- Scanners for understanding and interpretation of the text.
- Image preprocessing and segmentation of medical images, e.g., CT scans.
- Traffic analysis and real-time road processing by video segmentation and frame-by-frame image processing.
- Χλοσεδ-χιρχνιτ τελε℧ισιον (CCTV) cameras for traffic and crowd analytics

Table 7.1 presents a sample of problems in this area and algorithms used to solve them.

7.6 AUTOMATED ROBOTS AND DRONES

While most robots do not look like their pop culture representations, their capabilities are just as impressive. The

TABLE 7.1   Some Image Classification Tasks and Applied Algorithms

Item	Objective	Algorithm
1	Dimensionality reduction	DRL-based Q-learning
2	Applying dynamic policy in active learning	Dynamic policy
3	Learning the data selection criterion	Deep Q-learning, CNN (VGG-16), and ResNet.
4	Enhancing the classification when training samples are lacking	Few-shot learning
5	Solving the misclassification problem in the soft-attention mechanisms	DSFnet
6	Localizing the objects in scenes	Pre-trained CNN, -Deep Q-network
7	Detection of the objects in images using a hierarchical technique	Q-learning
8	Providing an Aesthetics Aware framework based on RL (A2-RL) to improve image cropping	LSTM
9	Providing a Fast Aesthetics-Aware Adversarial framework based on RL (Fast A3RL) to improve image cropping	LSTM and Adversarial learning
10	Providing a Fast Aesthetics-Aware Adversarial framework based on RL (Fast A3RL) to improve image cropping	Double DQN
11	Lightweight network for large-scale image classification with visual attention and Gaussian modeling	Redefined Markov process for RL with Gaussian distribution
12	Model for autonomous exploration of vehicles	Double deep Q-learning (DDQN), Faster R-CNN

more robots learn using RL, the more accurate they become, and the quicker they can complete a previously arduous task. They can also perform duties that would be dangerous for people with far less consequences. For these reasons, aside from requiring some oversight and regular maintenance, robots are a cost-effective and efficient alternative to manual labor.

Some more examples of RL in this area include the use of robots to:

- Deliver food to tables in restaurants.
- Identify lower shelves in grocery stores and order more products.
- Assemble products and inspect for defects in factories.
- Count, track, and manage inventory.
- Deliver goods.
- Travel long and short distances.
- Input, organize, and report on data.
- Grasp and handle objects of all different shapes and sizes.

The list is nonexhaustive. As we continue to test robotic abilities, new features are being added to expand their potential.

These successes show the ability of DRL to control robotic systems with high-dimensional state or observation space with highly nonlinear dynamics. Some of the tasks are highly challenging, which cannot be handled by conventional decision-making, planning, and control approaches.

The achievements of DRL have been mostly in simulation or game environments. Extending them to physical world presents additional challenges.

i. Collection of trial-and-error samples directly in the physical world is often inefficient and/or unsafe for the RL agents.

ii. It is usually impossible to simulate the complex real world exactly.

Still progress has been made in applying DRL to many physical environments, e.g., champion-level drone racing, quadruped locomotion control integrated into production-level quadruped systems (e.g., ANYbotics, Swiss-Mile, and Boston Dynamics), etc.

Some areas have seen rapid progress in applying DRL:

- *Locomotion*: DRL has enabled mature quadruped locomotion control. Hardware accessibility is an important contributing factor. Even in the mature quadruped locomotion domain, open questions remain, such as:

  i. Effectively integrating locomotion with downstream tasks via RL

  ii. Enabling efficient and safe real-world learning.

- *Navigation*: DRL has shown potential for local planning, global exploration, and constructing end-to-end navigation solutions, but the solutions lack explainability and safety guarantees. Therefore, it has not been deployed widely.

  i. *Visual navigation*: While end-to-end RL excels in simulation, most real-world successes deploy modular designs and learn components of the navigation stack. Joint reasoning jointly with navigation and locomotion enables agile legged and aerial navigation. Model-free, end-to-end policies show promise for structured indoor environments like homes, while modular architectures boost performance without sacrificing guarantees and generalization. RL-based vision-and-language navigation is relatively underexplored in real-world settings but promising given the recent advances in vision-language models.

  ii. *Legged navigation*: For agile legged and aerial navigation, jointly learning navigation and locomotion yields promising results. Yet, involving locomotion complicates the training of long-horizon navigation policies.

- Manipulation: DRL has been applied to both stationary and dynamic manipulation tasks like pick-and-place, contact-rich manipulation, in-hand manipulation, and non-prehensile manipulation. Stationary manipulation refers to an agent's control of its environment through selective contact. Robots require manipulation capabilities such as pick-and-place, mechanical assembly, in-hand manipulation, non-prehensile manipulation, etc., to be useful. Manipulation poses several challenges for both analytical and learning-based methods, as the mechanics of contact are complex and difficult to model, and open-world manipulation requires strong generalization and fast online learning. It poses fundamental difficulties for RL:

  a. Large observation and action spaces make real-world exploration prohibitively time-consuming and unsafe.
  b. Reward function design requires domain knowledge.
  c. Tasks are often long-horizon.
  d. Instantaneous environment resets are usually unrealistic in real-world tasks.

- Despite these challenges, RL has achieved notable successes in domains where the space of tasks is more constrained – grasping, in-hand manipulation, and assembly – rather than less, e.g., end-to-end pick-and-place. These more constrained tasks allow for a priori reward design and zero-shot sim-to-real transfer, whereas open-world pick-and-place and contact-rich manipulation require generalizing to diverse objects and tasks. The limitations of physical simulation may also preclude scaling sim-to-real for contact-rich tasks.

7.7 NATURAL LANGUAGE PROCESSING (NLP)

NLP tasks are some of the most important uses of RL. Some examples include:

- Text prediction,
- Text summarization,
- Question answering,
- Machine translation, etc.

RL agents train with patterns in texts and speech, and then mimic the language, diction, and syntax people speak to each other every day.

In NLP, the goal is to develop computer programs capable of communicating with humans using natural language. As an example, machine translation helps humans speaking different languages to understand each other by translating from one natural language to another. Over the years, NLP research has been transformed by ML algorithms and deep neural networks as neural language models such as BERT and various versions of GPT. These new approaches define natural languages as probability distributions over sentences rather than using definitive sets specified by grammars.

An important NLP approach uses n-grams, which is a sequence of written symbols of length n. The n-gram model is the probability distribution of n-grams defined as Markov chain of length n-1. The DNNs, such as the recurrent long short-term memory (LSTM) network, have allowed the researchers to replace probabilistic language models with those based on DNNs. The LSTM has been successfully applied to machine translation which was not possible with the approach based on language grammars alone. These new neural models contain thousands of parameters that are estimated iteratively from a massive number of training examples gathered from the Internet.

There are five main categories of MDP-based NLP problems.

i. *Conversational systems*: They are the most studied ones, and they involve finding an optimal dialog policy that should be followed by an automated system during a conversation with a human user. A very important advancement in this area occurred in 2016, when researchers from Stanford University, Ohio State University, and Microsoft Research used RL to generate dialogues using two RL agents. They applied policy gradient methods to reward coherence, informativity, and ease of answering in simulated conversations. The outcome has been adopted very widely in business customer service departments. The other four categories also use RL methods. In some of them, it is even not easy to identify the elements of a well-defined MDP.

ii. *Syntactic parsing*: It consists of analyzing a string made of symbols belonging to some alphabet, either in natural or in programming languages, using a set of rules called grammar. There could be many ways to perform parsing, depending on the final goal of the system, e.g., construction of a compiler for a new programming language, an application of language understanding for human–computer interaction, etc. A grammar can generate many parsing trees and each of these trees specifies the valid structure for sentences of the corresponding language. Since parsing can be represented as a sequential search problem with a parse tree as the final goal state, RL methods are tools well suited for the underlying sequential decision problem. In general, a parse is obtained as a path when an optimal policy is used in each MDP.

iii. *Language understanding*: It can also be posed as an MDP and therefore RL algorithms can be applied.

Furthermore, they can be implemented together with DNN to cope with the massive amount of data that text understanding applications typically require.

iv. *Text generation systems*: They automatically generate valid sentences in natural language given a language model. The optimization generates valid substring sequences that subsequently complete a whole sentence with some meaning in the domain of the application. For example, given a vector representation of a set of variables in a computational system and their corresponding values, an RL algorithm generates a sentence in English (or any other natural language). This communicates specific and meaningful information to a human user.

Generating navigational instructions for humans has been one of the first areas for this approach. Here, the system decides first the content to be communicated to the human, and then builds the correct instructions adding word by word. The reward function is implemented as a hidden Markov model or as a Bayesian network. The RL process is carried out with a hierarchical algorithm using semi-MDPs. Other approaches combining IRL and GANs have also been used in which the reward and the policy functions are learned alternately with a discriminator and a generator.

In a text generation task, the corresponding MDP works as follows:

a. Each state is a feature vector describing the current state of the system containing enough information to generate the output string.

b. Actions add or delete words.

c. Every transition to next state is determined by the resulting string, after adding or deleting a word.

d. The reward function is learned from a corpus of labeled data or from human feedback.

v. *Machine translation*: It consists in automatically translating sentences from one natural language to another one using a computing device with a program. It receives text (or speech) in some language as input and automatically generates text (or speech), with the same meaning in a different language. They are used mostly as online translation systems. Neural machine translation is the preferred approach now in which large NNs predict the likelihood of a sequence of words.

Currently RNN, such as LSTM network, is the preferred MT method. Two RNNs function as an encoder and a decoder:

a. The encoder updates its weights as it receives a sequence of input words to extract the meaning of the sentence. It internally encodes the meaning of the source text.

b. The decoder updates its corresponding weights to generate the correct sequence of output words of the translated sentence. It decodes using an internal representation and outputs a translated sentence with the correct meaning.

RL has been used to tackle the problems of exposure bias, i.e., the discrepancy between ground-truth-dependent prediction during training and model-output-dependent prediction during testing, and inconsistency between the training and test objectives.

7.8 SOME OTHER AREAS

RL methods are being used in a wide variety of areas in addition to those mentioned above. Some of them are:

a. Finding the ways to reduce energy consumption especially in data centers. Google achieved a 40% reduction in energy spending without the need for human intervention by developing RL and AI methods for this purpose. The steps in achieving energy reduction are the following:

- DNN using DRL is fed snapshots of data from the data centers every five minutes.
- DNN predicts future energy consumptions for different combinations of the data.
- System identifies actions leading to minimal power consumption subject to a set standard of safety criteria.
- These actions are implemented in the data center.
- The local control system verifies the actions.

A similar approach is used in setting the thermostat or the level of light in the room.

b. In trading, one tries to predict future prices of stocks before deciding whether to buy or sell. RL agents help in this by optimizing the buy/sell action for maximizing the future monetary reward based on the current state of knowledge. The optimization must consider factors like availability of money, risk appetite, and access to relevant information.

The entry of RL agents has also encouraged very fast real-time trading using dueling RL agents for making short-term profits. Only the future will tell if this use of RL is good for attaining socially desirable ends like decreasing inequality.

c. Climate change, poverty and inequality, responsible wealth generation and resource management, education, government, and military are some of the areas in which RL methods have been found to be very useful.

Epilogue

THE IDEA OF REINFORCEMENT learning combined with neural network has revolutionized the field of machine learning. It has led to an explosion of applications in several fields of social and scientific importance. It is difficult to forecast the future of RL but certainly we can look forward to more and more exciting applications of this seminal idea in near future.

Like many scientific and technological applications, RL can be also used for unsavory ends that harm individuals and societies. We must exert our utmost effort to prevent this and, in cases where this is not possible, at least to minimize repercussions. That is easier said than done as it will involve widespread collective awareness and social effort.

In the future, we can envision the areas of application of RL expanding to solve more and more social and scientific problems. It will be one of the most widely available tools in the hands of researchers as well as decision-makers. Let us hope that it will help in solving some of the pressing problems currently facing humanity, like environmental degradation and inequality.

Acknowledgments

I THANK NOAH WESTON FOR suggesting exploring the area of machine learning. I also want to acknowledge the stimulating discussions on RL with Professors Jay Kuo (University of Southern California) and Mani Srivastava (University of California at Los Angeles) and my colleagues Peng Wang and Venkat Dasari.

Bibliography

Books

1. *Deep Reinforcement Learning*, by Aske Plaat, arxiv: 2201.02135
2. *Auto-Encoding Variational Bayes*, by D. Kingma and M. Welling, arXiv:1312.6114v11 [stat.ML] 10 Dec 2022
3. *Reinforcement Learning for Generative AI: State of the Art, Opportunities and Open Research Challenges*, by Giorgio Franceschelli and Mirco Musolesi, arXiv:2308.00031v4 [cs. LG] 8 Feb 2024

Reviews and Surveys

1. "Deep Reinforcement Learning: An Overview", Yuxi Li (yuxili@gmail.com), arXiv: 1701.07274v6 [cs.LG]
2. "Deep Learning: A Comprehensive Overview on Techniques, Taxonomy, Applications and Research Directions", Iqbal H. Sarker, *SN Computer Science* 2, 420, 2021. https://doi.org/ 10.1007/s42979-021-00815-1
3. "Towards Data-and Knowledge-Driven Artificial Intelligence: A Survey on Neuro-Symbolic Computing", Wenguan Wang and Yi Yang, arXiv:2210.15889v1 [cs.AI], 28 Oct 2022
4. "Symbolic and Statistical Theories of Cognition: Towards Integrated Artificial Intelligence", Maruyama, Y., *International Conference on Software Engineering and Formal Methods* 129(146), 2020.

5. "A Comprehensive Survey of Loss Functions in Machine Learning", Qi Wang, Yue Ma, Kun Zhao, and Yingjie Tian, *Annals of Data Science* 9, 187–212, 2022. https://doi.org/10.1007/s40745-020-00253-51 3
6. "Loss Functions", Sparsh Gupta, https://builtin.com/machine-learning/common-loss-functions, Apr. 17, 2022.
7. "Physics-Informed Neural Networks: A Deep Learning Framework for Solving Forward and Inverse Problems Involving Nonlinear Partial Differential Equations", M. Raissi, P. Perdikaris, and G.E. Karniadakis, *Journal of Computational Physics* 378, 686–707, 2019.
8. "A Mathematical Theory of Communication", C. E. Shannon, *The Bell System Technical Journal* 27, 379–423, 623–656, July, October, 1948.
9. arXiv: 1612.03365 Multi-Instance Learning Survey.
10. arXiv: 1701.07274 DRL Overview.

Other Materials

1. www.quantamagazine.org/artificial-neural-nets-finally-yield-clues-to-how-brains-learn-20210218/
2. https://bdtechtalks.com/2020/06/22/direct-fit-artificial-neural-networks/
3. www.nature.com/articles/d41586-019-02212-4
4. https://towardsdatascience.com/the-differences-between-artificial-and-biological-neural-networks-a8b46db828b7
5. https://searchenterpriseai.techtarget.com/feature/How-neural-network-training-methods-are-modeled-after-the-human-brain
6. www.nature.com/articles/s41467-019-11786-6
7. "Can Artificial Intelligence Replicate the Human Brain?", Genevieve Hayes, https://blogs.oracle.com/ai-and-datascience/post/reinforcement-learning-proximal-policy-optimization-ppo
8. "What Is Generative AI? Everything You Need to Know" (techtarget.com), George Lawton, June 2023.

9. "Physics-Informed Model-Based Reinforcement Learning", Adithya Ramesh and Balaraman Ravindran, arXiv:2212.02179v4 [cs.LG] 14 May 2023.

10. "Physics-informed Reinforcement Learning for Perception and Reasoning about Fluids", Beatriz Moya, Alberto Badias, David Gonzalez, Francisco Chinesta, and Elias Cueto, arXiv: 2203.05775v1 [cs.CV], 11 Mar 2022.

11. "Explainable AI: Current Status and Future Directions", P GOHEL et al., arXiv:2107.07045v1 [cs.LG], 12 Jul 2021.

12. "Quantum Machine Learning", Wikipedia.

13 "A Survey on Quantum Reinforcement Learning", Nico Meyer, Christian Ufrecht, Maniraman Periyasamy, Daniel D. Scherer, Axel Plinge, and Christopher Mutschler, arXiv:2211.03464v1 [quant-ph], 7 Nov 2022.

14. "Variational Quantum Circuits for Deep Reinforcement Learning", Samuel Yen-Chi Chen, Chao-Han Huck Yang, Jun Qi, Pin-Yu Chen, Xiaoli Ma, and Hsi-Sheng Goan, arXiv:1907.00397v3 [cs.LG], 20 Jul 2020.

15. "Physics-Guided, Physics-Informed, and Physics-Encoded Neural Networks in Scientific Computing", Salah A. Faroughia, Nikhil M. Pawara, Ceelio Fernandes, Maziar Raissi, Subasish Das, Nima K. Kalantarie, and Seyed Kourosh Mahjour, arxiv [cs. LG] 2211.07377v2, 2022.

16. "Formal Algorithms for Transformers", Mary Phuong and Marcus Hutter (DeepMind), arXiv: 2207.09238v1, 2022.

17. "One Small Step for Generative AI, One Giant Leap for AGI: A Complete Survey on ChatGPT in AIGC Era", Chaoning Zhang et al., arXiv:2304.06488v1 [cs. CY], 2303.

18. "A Complete Survey on Generative AI (AIGC): Is ChatGPT from GPT-4 to GPT-5 All You Need?", Chaoning Zhang et al., arXiv:2303.11717, 2023.

19. "Scientists' Perspectives on the Potential for Generative AI in Their Fields", Meredith Ringel Morris, arXiv: 2304.01420v1, 2023.
20. www.analyticsvidhya.com/blog/2020/11/entropy-a-key-concept-for-all-data-science-beginners/
21. https://theaisummer.com/Deep_Q_Learning/
22. www.rebellionresearch.com/convolutional-neural-network-explained
23. https://medium.com/analytics-vidhya/activation-functions-all-you-need-to-know-355a850d025e
24. www.mathworks.com/help/reinforcement-learning/ug/td3-agents.html
25. https://spinningup.openai.com/en/latest/algorithms/ppo.html
26. https://machinelearningmastery.com/how-to-code-the-generative-adversarial-network-training-algorithm-and-loss-functions/
27. https://spinningup.openai.com/en/latest/algorithms/trpo.html
28. www.v7labs.com/blog/deep-reinforcement-learningguide#:~:text=There%20are%20two%20main%20types%20of%20Reinforcement%20Learning,1%201.%20Model-based%20algorithms%202%202.%20Model-free%20algorithms
29. https://en.wikipedia.org/wiki/Long_short-term_memory
30. https://towardsdatascience.com/inductive-vs-transductive-learning-e608e786f7d
31. "Variational Autoencoder", Wikipedia.
32. "A Cookbook of Self-Supervised Learning", Randall Balestriero et al., arXiv:2304.12210v2 [cs.LG], 28 Jun 2023.
33. "Activation Functions — All You Need To Know!", Sukanya Bag, Feb 13, 2021. https://medium.com/analytics-vidhya/activation-functions-all-you-need-to-know-355a850d025e
34. "A Survey of Information Entropy Metrics for Complex Networks", Yamila M. Omar and Peter Plapper, Entropy 2020, 22, 1417; doi:10.3390/e22121417

35. "Learning Diverse Skills via Maximum Entropy Deep Reinforcement Learning", Haoran Tang and Tuomas Haarnoja, https://bair.berkeley.edu/blog/2017/10/06/soft-q-learning/

36. Solution to BE arXiv:quant-ph/0407192v2, 21 Mar 2005.

37. 9 Deep Reinforcement Learning | The Mathematical Engineering of Deep Learning (2021) (deeplearningmath. org).

38. "Multi-agent Reinforcement Learning: A Comprehensive Survey", Dom Huh and Prasant Mohapatra, arXiv:2312.10256v2 [cs.MA], 3 Jul 2024.

39. "A Survey on Multi-Agent Deep Reinforcement Learning: From the Perspective of Challenges and Applications", Wei Du and Shifei Ding, *Artificial Intelligence Review* 54, 3215–3238, 2021. https://doi.org/10.1007/s10 462-020-09938-y

40. "Reinforcement Learning with Reward Machines in Stochastic Games", Jueming Hu et al., arXiv:2305.17372v3 [cs.MA], 28 Aug 2023.

41. "Reward Machines for Cooperative Multi-Agent Reinforcement Learning", Cyrus Neary, Zhe Xu, Bo Wu, and Ufuk Topcu, arXiv:2007.01962 [cs.MA]

42. "MultiAgent Deep Reinforcement Learning: A Survey", Sven Gronauer and Klaus Diepold.

43. "A Practical Guide to Multi-Objective Reinforcement Learning and Planning", Conor F. Hayes et al., arXiv:2103.09568v1 [cs.AI], 17 Mar 2021.

44. "Neurosymbolic AI – Why, What, and How", Amit Sheth, Kaushik Roy, and Manas Gaur, arXiv:2305.00813v1 [cs. AI], 1 May 2023.

45. "Multi-Agent Deep Reinforcement Learning", Maxim Egorov, Stanford University; Zhang, H. and Yu, T. (2020). "Taxonomy of Reinforcement Learning Algorithms", In: Dong, H., Ding, Z., and Zhang, S. (Eds), *Deep Reinforcement Learning*. Springer, Singapore. https://doi. org/10.1007/978-981-15-4095-0_3

46. "Reinforcement Learning Algorithms: An Overview and Classification", Fadi AlMahamid and Katarina Grolinger, arXiv:2209.14940v1 [cs.LG], 29 Sep 2022.

47. "Introduction to Multi-Arm Bandits", Slivkins, Aleksandrs. https://arxiv.org/pdf/1904.07272.pdf

48. SOM algorithm. https://towardsdatascience.com/self-org anizing-maps-1b7d2a84e065

49. *Continuous Deep Q-Learning with Model-based Acceleration*", Shixiang Gu, Timothy Lillicrap, Ilya Sutskever, Sergey Levine, arXiv: 1603.00748v1 [cs.LG], 2 Mar 2016.

50. How to Code the GAN Training Algorithm and Loss Functions – MachineLearningMastery.compseudo_code_ lstm.py at Github

51. Tutorial on LSTMs: A Computational Perspective | by Manu Rastogi | Towards Data Science.

52. "LSTM: A Search Space Odyssey", Klaus Greff, Rupesh K. Srivastava, Jan Koutnˊık, Bas R. Steunebrink, and Jˆurgen Schmidhuber, arXiv:1503.04069v2 [cs.NE], 4 Oct 2017.

53. Long short-term memory – Wikipedia.

54. Proximal Policy Optimization — Spinning Up Documentation (openai.com).

55. Proximal Policy Optimization — Spinning Up Documentation (openai.com).

56. Trust Region Policy Optimization — Spinning Up Documentation (openai.com).

57. TD3: Learning to Run with AI. Learn to build one of the most powerful… | by Donal Byrne | Towards Data Science.

58. Twin-Delayed Deep Deterministic (TD3) Policy Gradient Agents – MATLAB & Simulink (mathworks.com).

59. Deep Deterministic Policy Gradient — Spinning Up Documentation (openai.com).

60. https://towardsdatascience.com/in-depth-review-of-soft-actor-critic-91448aba63d4 Chris Yoon.

61. *"Continuous Deep Q-Learning with Model-based Acceleration"*, Shixiang Gu, Timothy Lillicrap, Ilya Sutskever, and Sergey Levine, arXiv: 1603.00748v1 [cs.LG] 2 Mar 2016.

62. https://towardsdatascience.com/policy-gradients-in-a-nutshell-8b72f9743c5d

63. *"Connecting Generative Adversarial Networks and Actor-Critic Methods"*, Pfau, David and Oriol Vinyals, arXiv preprint arXiv:1610.01945 (2016).

64. "Review of Deep Reinforcement Learning", Keyuan Yu, Kun Jin2, and Xiangyang Deng, IEEE IMCEC ISSN:2693-2776.

65. www.datacamp.com/tutorial/comprehensive-introduction-graph-neural-networks-gnns-tutorial

66. "Deep Reinforcement Learning Meets Graph Neural Networks: Exploring a Routing Optimization Use Case", Paul Almasan, Jos´e Su´arez-Varela, Krzysztof Rusek, Pere Barlet-Ros, and Albert Cabellos-Aparicio, arXiv:1910.07421v3 [cs.NI], 7 Oct 2022.

67. "Explainable Reinforcement Learning (XRL): A Systematic Literature Review and Taxonomy", Yanzhe Bekkemoen, *Machine Learning* 113, 355–441, 2024. https://doi.org/10.1007/s10994-023-06479-7)

68. "Deep Reinforcement Learning for Autonomous Driving: A Survey", B Ravi Kiran, Ibrahim Sobh, Victor Talpaert, Patrick Mannion, Ahmad A. Al Sallab, Senthil Yogamani, and Patrick Pérez, arXiv:2002.00444v2 [cs.LG], 23 Jan 2021.

69. "Reinforcement Learning in Healthcare: A Survey", Chao Yu, Jiming Liu, Fellow, IEEE, and Shamim Nemati, arXiv:1908.08796v4 [cs.LG], 24 Apr 2020.

70. "An Extensive Review of Applications, Methods and Recent Advances in Deep Reinforcement Learning", Shiva Shashank Dhavala, C. Srihari, R. Rashmi and K. Vanishree, *5th International Congress on Human-Computer Interaction,*

Optimization and Robotic Applications (HORA), 2023. DOI: 10.1109/HORA58378.2023.10156687

71. "Survey on Reinforcement Learning for Language Processing", Victor Uc-Cetina, Nicolas Navarro-Guerrero, Anabel Martin-Gonzalez, Cornelius Weber, and Stefan Wermter, arXiv:2104.05565v3 [cs.CL], 15 Mar 2022.

72. "Deep Reinforcement Learning for Robotics: A Survey of Real-World Successes", Chen Tang, Ben Abbatematteo, Jiaheng Hu, Rohan Chandra, Roberto Mart´in-Mart´in, and Peter Stone, arXiv:2408.03539v3 [cs.RO], 16 Sep 2024.

73. "Reinforcement Learning in Image Classification: A Review", Norah Alrebdi, Sarah Alrumiah, Atheer Almansour, and Murad Rassam, *2022 2nd International Conference on Computing and Information Technology (ICCIT),* Jan. 25 – 27, 2022.

74. "A Survey on Quantum Reinforcement Learning", Nico Meyer, Christian Ufrecht, Maniraman Periyasamy, Daniel D. Scherer, Axel Plinge, and Christopher Mutschler, arXiv:2211.03464v2 [quant-ph], 8 Mar 2024.

75. Reinforcement learning from human feedback – Wikipedia.

76. https://medium.com/geekculture/binary-neural-netwo rks-a-game-changer-in-machine-learning-6ae0013d3dcb

Index

For Product Safety Concerns and Information please contact our EU
representative GPSR@taylorandfrancis.com
Taylor & Francis Verlag GmbH, Kaufingerstraße 24, 80331 München, Germany